Copyright ©

ISBN 978-0-915545-17-9
First Printing 2014

Printed in the United States of America
All Rights Reserved!

Published by
Stanley R. Abbott Ministries, Inc.
P.O. Box 533
McRae, Georgia 31055
U.S.A.

Birthed into the Supernatural

Preface

In the late 1800's a wonderful tale flowed out of the mind of Mark Twain onto the pages of a novel entitled **The Prince and the Pauper.** In this story two boys discovered they were identical in appearance and determined to change places with one another for a season to experience life from the other's perspective. One of the boys was Prince Edward, son of King Henry VIII, the other Tom Canty, a pauper and son of an abusive drunken father. The difficulties which ensued were monumental. King Henry VIII died, and Tom Canty was about to be crowned King of England. Finally, Edward's true identity was established allowing him to regain his rightful place to be crowned King instead of Tom.

Imagine if we were actually princes destined in some dispensation to reign as *"...kings and priests to our God..." (Revelation 5:9,10)* but living as paupers. Imagine all of the horrors of our lives as paupers were direct results of mistaken or misplaced identity. The similarities between the theme of Twain's novel and the condition of the church on the earth today are striking.

You and I have been born again with God Himself as our Father *(John 1:11-13)*. We have become *"...members of the household of God..." (Ephesians 2:19)*. We have been baptized into Christ as flesh and bone parts of His body *(Ephesians 5:30-32)*. We have the same Spirit who raised Jesus from the dead living inside of us *(Romans 8:11)*. We are ordained to live as Jesus lived *(I John 2:6)* and to do the works Jesus did *(John 14:12)*.

We must escape from our captivity and take our rightful place in the household of our Father. ***How do we do that? Jesus is our way!*** This book provides a modicum of revelation as only one small piece necessary to help us move out of our old traditions into the new covenant!

Birthed into the Supernatural

Table of Contents

Chapter One
Born Again 1 - 10

Chapter Two
Birthed into the Kingdom of God 11 - 20

Chapter Three
Growth in the Kingdom 21 - 30

Chapter Four
Living Like Jesus 31 - 40

Chapter Five
Transformation 41 - 50

Chapter Six
Submission to Live 51 - 60

Birthed into the Supernatural

Chapter Seven
Deception Undetected   61 - 70

Chapter Eight
Eternal Fundamentals   71 - 88

Conclusion   89 - 92

Chapter One

Born Again

You must be born again! These are most definitely extraordinary, exotic, even impossible words. The notion they represent is beyond human belief and ability. Nicodemus, a ruler of the Jews, came to Jesus by night to inquire of the Lord *(John 3:1-21)*. Jesus' words to Nicodemus began with the revelation of being born again. The foundational basis for being born again is so far beyond anything natural man is capable of understanding, much less accepting, we must have help from God to understand.

There is a phenomenon in the natural world involving human language. Words interpreted a certain way and spoken over a long period of time can cause their true meaning to be obscured by man's familiarity with them. A natural example would be the use of the term *"...coke..."* in the deep South. This term has become a generic representative for all soft drinks. If we ask a person if they want a *"...coke..."*, it is typically not a specific reference to the product *"...Coca Cola..."*, but to any soft drink. We must avoid this phenomenon when considering the Word of God. Familiarity with God's word must not cause His word to lose the meaning He intended for it to have.

Being *"...born again..."* provides us with a spiritual example of this phenomenon. This saying *"...born again..."*

Birthed into the Supernatural

gained popularity, even some degree of acceptance, by people of the world when politically and socially celebrated individuals began to use the saying in relation to their own lives. Being born again began to be interpreted as a *"...saying..."* signifying a person's religious preference as Christian. However, being born again is so much more than a saying signifying preference of religion.

Nicodemus said to Jesus, *"...Rabbi, we know that You are a teacher come from God; for no one can do these signs that You do unless God is with him..." (John 3:2)*. Immediately, without any other dialogue, Jesus replied, *"... 'Most assuredly, I say to you, unless one is born again, he cannot see the kingdom of God'..." (John 3:3)*. Did Jesus just change the subject matter, ignoring Nicodemus' words, or was His reply a direct response to what Nicodemus had said? We need to discover which one.

An incident involving Paul while he was under house arrest in Rome adds needed information to our quest. He had opportunity to minister to many people from his lodging. On one occasion after he had called the leaders of the Jews together, he told them the reason he had gathered them was because of his hope for Israel. They agreed to hear Paul further. On a certain day many came to hear what he had to say. After Paul had spoken from morning till evening words regarding the kingdom of God, *"...some were persuaded by the things which were spoken, and some disbelieved..." (Acts 28:24)*.

When Paul saw them disagreeing among themselves, he quoted a prophetic word Isaiah had spoken to their Jewish fathers. After Paul had quoted the prophesy given by Isaiah, the Jews departed from him.

> *"Go to this people and say; hearing you will hear, and shall not understand; and seeing you will see, and not perceive; for the hearts of this people have grown dull. Their ears are hard of hearing, and their eyes they have closed, lest they should see with their eyes and hear with their ears, lest they should understand with their hearts and turn, so that I should heal them."* **Acts 28:26,27**
>
> *(Scripture quoted from **Isaiah 6:9,10**)*

Scripture is teaching us it is possible for a people to have God's provisions made available to them but still not be able to see, hear, or understand what is set before them.

Now, back to our unanswered question whether Jesus changed the subject matter in His response to Nicodemus' comments *(John 3:2,3)*. Jesus did not change the subject matter in his conversation with Nicodemus. He was offering Nicodemus a way to see Him and His ministry in a way that he could not have otherwise been able to see. He was offering him opportunity *"...to **know how** to see the kingdom of God..."*! Jesus told him, *"...unless one is born again, he cannot see the kingdom of God..."*. Because of Jesus' love for Nicodemus, He was opening the door for him to be born again so he could *"...see the kingdom of God..."* and partake of eternal life.

Being born again is not a saying signifying a person's religious preference. It is God's provision for a person to be able *"...to see the kingdom of God..."* and become a flesh and bone part of Christ's body, *"...the church..."*. All born again people are not merely members of a church. *Together with Christ, we are the church!* The difference between just being members of a church and being the church is huge.

It is impossible for natural man to understand the meaning of *"...born again..."*. When Jesus introduced this revelation to Nicodemus, Nicodemus immediately began considering what possible meaning these words could have, reasoning with his natural mind. It's as if he was thinking out loud...

> '*...How can a man be born when he is old? Can he enter a second time into his mother's womb and be born?'...*" **John 3:4**

It is vitally important to continually remind ourselves *"...with man..."* everything in the kingdom of God *"...is impossible..."*, but *"...with God, all things are possible..."*.

In only two verses Jesus provides the foundation required for Nicodemus to begin to shift his thoughts from natural to spiritual in order for him to begin to understand the meaning of *"...born again..."*

> '*...Most assuredly, I say to you, unless one is born of water and the Spirit, he cannot enter the kingdom of God. That which is born of the flesh is flesh, and that which is born of the Spirit is spirit.'...*" **John 3:5,6**

Being born again is *not* oriented to the natural world but rather the spiritual world. When a person is born again, his spirit is the target for his new birth, not his flesh.

Born Again

But why does man's spirit need to be born again?

Adam's life in the Garden of Eden points us in the right direction to find the answers we seek.

> *"Then the Lord God took the man and put him in the garden of Eden to tend and keep it. And the Lord God commanded the man, saying,*
>
> > *'Of every tree of the garden you may freely eat; but of the tree of the knowledge of good and evil you shall not eat, for in the day you eat of it you shall surely die.'*
>
> **Genesis 2:15-17**

According to this Scripture the Lord told Adam he would die the day he ate the fruit of the tree of the knowledge of good and evil. Yet three chapters later Scripture says Adam begat sons, daughters, and lived to the age of nine hundred and thirty years before he died *(Genesis 5:1-5)*. The immediate death of which the Lord said Adam would partake, *"...the tree of the knowledge of good and evil you shall not eat, for in the day you eat of it you shall surely die...",* must have a meaning other than just natural physical death.

Before Adam disobeyed God and ate the forbidden fruit, his spirit was actively connected with God. He walked with God. He had dominion from God to rule over all the works of God's hands. After Adam disobeyed, everything changed between him and God. Dominion was taken away from him. From that point, instead of Adam having divinely empowered abilities, he was only left with his own abilities as a mere man.

Birthed into the Supernatural

"Then to Adam He (God) said,

> *'Because you have heeded the voice of your wife, and have eaten from the tree of which I commanded you, saying You shall not eat of it; Cursed is the ground for your sake; in toil you shall eat of it all the days of your life. both thorns and thistles it shall bring forth for you, and you shall eat the herb of the field. In the sweat of your face you shall eat bread till you return to the ground, for out of it you were taken; for dust you are, and to dust you shall return...'*

Genesis 3:17-19

Adam was stripped of divinely empowered abilities, stripped of his dominion, kept from partaking of the fruit from the tree of life, had to live on earth now cursed as a result of his disobedience, driven out of the garden of Eden, and lost intimate access to and relationship with God *(Genesis 3:1-24)*. All of these things equate to spiritual death. Adam suffered all of these things the day he disobeyed God.

God's will was for mankind to have divinely empowered abilities, to have dominion, to partake of the fruit of eternal life, to live on a blessed earth, and to be able to *"...come to the Father..." (John 14:6)*. Even though the man Adam violated God's will and died spiritually losing all of these things, God's desire for man to have all these things never changed. From the fall of the first Adam to the coming of Jesus as the last Adam *(I Corinthians 15:35-49)*, God was making a way for man to be restored back to spiritual life *(Romans 5:12-21)* restoring access to Himself *(John 14:6)* and all that Adam lost.

Born Again

Scripture clearly states that man was created in the image of God *(Genesis 1:26)*. We accept by faith that our God is a Triune God made up of three separable and identifiable parts, yet One God. When Jesus *("...the Word became flesh and dwelt among us..." John 1:14)* was baptized in the River Jordan and came up from the water, John the Baptist saw *"...the Spirit of God descending like a dove and alighting upon Him..." (Matthew 3:16)* and heard a voice from heaven saying, *"...This is my beloved Son, in whom I am well pleased..."(Matthew 3:17 See also **Mark1:10,11; Luke 3:21,22; John 1:32-34)**.* Three separable and identifiable parts, yet one God.

Because God is three separable and identifiable parts, yet One God, then man must be three separable and identifiable parts, yet one person, too. We are spirit, soul, and body. Mankind propagates our species through procreation. Human procreation involves giving birth to offspring. When a child is born, he is comprised of a spirit, a soul, and a body, three separable and identifiable parts, yet one person.

In Paul's letter to the church at Rome he revealed how sin and death came into the earth and was passed on to all men.

> "Therefore, as through one man's (Adam's) offense judgment came to all men, resulting in condemnation, even so through one Man's (Jesus') righteous act the free gift came to all men, resulting in justification of life. For as one man's disobedience many were made sinners, so also by one Man's obedience many will be made righteous. Moreover the law entered that the offense might abound.

Birthed into the Supernatural

> *But where sin abounded, grace abounded much more, so that as sin reigned in death, even so grace might reign through righteousness to eternal life through Jesus Christ our Lord."* **Romans 5:19-21** *(See entire context in verses 12-21)*

The *"...man..."* Adam was stripped of divinely empowered abilities, stripped of his dominion, kept from partaking of the fruit from the tree of life, had to live on earth now cursed as a result of his disobedience, was driven out of the garden of Eden, and lost intimate access to and relationship with God. According to Paul's inspired letter to the church at Rome *(Romans 5:12-21)*, these conditions apply to all who are the offspring of men.

However, even though Adam violated God's will and was stripped of the quality of life he once had, God's desire for man to have divinely empowered abilities, to have dominion, to partake of the fruit of eternal life, to live on a blessed earth, and to be able to *"...come to the Father..." (John 14:6)* was not just for the man Adam, it was for all mankind. So He designed a plan which would make a way for mankind to be restored.

The spiritual death of which men partake as procreations of men must be removed. God's plan made a way for all men to be born again! Not like Nicodemus thought, *'...How can a man be born when he is old? Can he enter a second time into his mother's womb and be born?'..." (John 3:4)*, but as Jesus revealed, *'...Most assuredly, I say to you, unless one is born of water and the Spirit, he cannot enter the kingdom of God. That which is born of the flesh is

Born Again

flesh, and that which is born of the Spirit is spirit.'..." *(John 3:5,6)*. Jesus became the doorway through which man by being born again could *"...come to the Father..." (John 10:1-19; John 14:6)!* New birth gave man a way to be reconciled with God *(II Corinthians 5:17-21)* which would restore all that Adam lost to all who would be reconciled with God.

Birthed into the Supernatural

Chapter Two

Birthed into the Kingdom of God

In order for Jesus to be birthed into the kingdom of men, he had to first be conceived as a human child, grow to term, and go through the birthing process required for all men. The conception part of this process has significant relevance to our birth into the kingdom of God.

The virgin Mary, who conceived Jesus, had a visitation from the angel Gabriel. When the angel told Mary she was going to conceive the child Jesus, Mary was incredulous. She asked how this was possible since she had never had relations with a man. The angel gave her a direct and very specific answer...

> "...*The Holy Spirit will come upon you, and the power of the Highest will overshadow you; therefore, also, that Holy One who is to be born will be called the Son of God.* Now indeed, Elizabeth your relative has also conceived a son in her old age; and this is now the sixth month for her who was called barren. For with God nothing will be impossible..." **Luke 1:35-37**

Since "*...faith comes by hearing, and hearing by the word of God...*" *(Romans 10:17)*, the angel included the word about Mary's cousin Elizabeth's supernatural conception, adding "*...with God nothing will be impossible...*". The angel was providing ample word from God, so Mary's faith would be sufficiently based. Mary's reply was simple and faith filled demonstrating a holy submission to the word from God spoken through the angel Gabriel.

> *"...Behold the maidservant of the Lord! Let it be to me according to your word..."* **Luke 1:38**

In order for conception to have taken place in the virgin Mary, three things were required:

1. *Seed of the word from God regarding conception had to be planted in her from which Jesus could be conceived.*

2. *Mary had to receive and submit to the word as a word from God.*

3. *The Holy Spirit had to be involved in order to transform the seed of the word into the human element necessary for conception to take place.*

We see three extremely similar things involved in the salvation experience for man. The first two can be seen in Paul's letter to the church at Rome.

> *"...whoever calls on the name of the Lord shall be saved. How then shall they call on Him in whom they have not believed? And how shall they believe in Him of whom they have not heard? And how shall they hear without a preacher? And how shall they preach unless they are sent?...So then faith comes by hearing, and hearing by the word of God."* **Romans 10:13-15 & 17**

Anyone can be saved simply by calling on the name of the Lord. In order to be able to call on the name of the Lord, a person must believe in the Lord. In order to believe in the Lord, a person must first have heard of the Lord. In order for

Birthed into the Kingdom

a person to hear of the Lord, someone must be sent to tell them about the Lord.

The third thing can be seen when Paul wrote about the involvement of the Holy Spirit for a person to be able to call Jesus Lord in his letter to the church at Corinth, *"...no one can say that Jesus is Lord except by the Holy Spirit..." (I Corinthians 12:3)*.

Our salvation experience causes us to be born again. John wrote a simple yet conclusive word in his gospel regarding our being *"...born..."* into the kingdom of God.

> *"He (Jesus) came unto His own, and His own did not receive Him. But as many as received Him, to them He gave the right to become children of God, to those who believe in His name; **who were born**, not of blood, nor of the will of the flesh, nor of the will of man, but of God." **John 1:11-13***

As in conception taking place in the virgin Mary, the three extremely similar things required for our salvation are:

1. *Seed of the word of God regarding salvation has to be planted in us from which Jesus can become our Lord.*

2. *We have to receive and submit to the word planted in us as the word from God.*

3. *The Holy Spirit has to be involved in order for us to call Jesus Lord.*

Being *"...born again..."* is as supernatural an event as Mary's virgin conception. It is extremely important for us to understand that when we were born again, we were

Birthed into the Supernatural

"...birthed..." into the kingdom of God. This birthing process actually made us children of God. God became our Father as surely as our earthly fathers are our fathers *(John 1:11-13)*.

Every natural child partakes of his natural father's nature. Our earthly fathers' DNA is our DNA. We are our fathers' sons. In a parallel manner when we were born again, we partook of our heavenly Father's nature. The implications of this *"...truth..."* are staggering for the lives we are to live after our new birth. In Peter's second epistle, what could easily be passed over as just his greeting to the church actually contains this truth about our having partaken of the divine nature.

> *"Simon Peter, a bondservant and apostle of Jesus Christ, to those who have obtained like precious faith with us by the righteousness of our God and Savior Jesus Christ: Grace and peace be multiplied to you in the knowledge of God and of Jesus our Lord, as His divine power has given to us all things that pertain to life and godliness, through the knowledge of Him who called us by glory and virtue, **by which have been given to us exceedingly great and precious promises, that through these you may be partakers of the divine nature**, having escaped the corruption that is in the world through lust."*
> **II Peter 1:1-4**

The spiritual environment for our sonship is unique and peculiar. Paul wrote about this environment most directly and simply in his letters to the churches at Ephesus and Galatia. In his letter to the church at Ephesus he compared the husband-wife role to Christ and the church.

Birthed into the Kingdom

> *"...So husbands ought to love their own wives as their own bodies; he who loves his wife loves himself. For no one ever hated his own flesh, but nourishes and cherishes it, just as the Lord does the church. 'For we are members of His body, of His flesh and of His bones. For this reason a man shall leave his father and mother and be joined to his wife, and the two shall become one flesh.' This is a great mystery, but I speak concerning Christ and the church."* **Ephesians 5:28-32**

The environment for our lives in the kingdom of God is inside the body of Christ as flesh of His flesh and bone of His bone. Our sonship was not designed to be lived independently of Christ but, rather, intimately united with Christ.

Paul's letter to the church at Galatia is even more dramatic in this matter if that is possible. Paul was writing to a troubled church who has been bewitched into believing their lives can be walked out as natural men in the power of their natural abilities. Paul was endeavoring to restore the church's understanding of their spiritual lives, which could only have been lived by faith. As Paul rehearsed these things, he wrote the promises of God were only made to Abraham and his Seed who is Christ and all who are Christ's by faith. We are Abraham's Seed.

> *"Now to Abraham and his Seed were the promises made, He does not say, 'And to seeds,' as of many, but as of one, 'And to your Seed,' who is Christ...For you are all sons of God through faith in Christ Jesus. For as many of you as were baptized into Christ have put on Christ. There is neither Jew nor Greek, there is neither slave nor free, there is neither male nor female; for you are all one in Christ Jesus. And **if you are Christ's, then you are Abraham's seed, and heirs according to the promise.**"* **Galatians 3:16 & 26-29** *(Context 3:1-4:7)*

Birthed into the Supernatural

The *"...divine nature..."* of which we have partaken and being *"...Abraham's Seed..."* are both only possible when we become Christ's! Baptized into Christ as flesh of His flesh and bone of His bone makes us Abraham's Seed. Scripture is very clear in this matter, *"...Now to Abraham and his Seed were the promises made, He does not say, And to seeds, as of many, but as of one, And to your Seed, who is Christ..."*. Everything we are and all that we have are a result of being Christ's! Understanding this truth is absolutely required for us to be able to live successfully in the kingdom of God.

No matter how true and how wonderful the truth is about our partaking of the *"...divine nature..."* or being *"...Abraham's Seed..."*, we all enter the kingdom the same way: by being born again. **Why is this significant?** The concept of natural world illustrations will help answer this question. Jesus often taught people during His earthly ministry by using natural world illustrations with which the people were familiar. He expected the people to use what they knew about the natural world illustrations and apply that understanding to what He was teaching them from the spirit world.

The Holy Spirit inspired use of a natural world concept, *"...to be born..."*, in conjunction with the spiritual world being *"...born again..."*. The concept of being born in the natural world is commonly understood by all. The process of life from birth to adulthood is also commonly understood. Every person who is born into the natural world is born as an infant. This is understood by all. Comparatively, in the spirit world, being *"...born again..."* births us into the kingdom of God as infants. Consider Peter's instructions to those who were newly born again.

Birthed into the Kingdom

"...as newborn babes, desire the pure milk of the word, that you may grow thereby..." **II Peter 2:2**

Our natural world understanding of newborn infants can easily be applied to the spirit world. A newborn in the natural world requires supervision and nourishment in order to grow successfully. Lack of either of these requirements can lead to great damage in the child, possibly even death. A newborn in the spirit world requires supervision and nourishment, too. Adequate supervision and nourishment are components completely necessary for the child's development in both the natural and spiritual worlds.

The dietary requirements for infants, either in the natural or spiritual world, are principally the same. Both require *"...milk..."* in order for the life the infants have been given to be sustained and for them to grow. The initial diet of an infant becomes the fundamental building block upon which the remainder of the child's life will be built, healthy or less than.

Pediatricians and nutritionists in the natural world are very particular about the milk of which an infant is to partake, the temperature of the milk, the frequency of intake, even the resulting number of urinations and defecations. Growth of the infant is carefully monitored by parents and physicians to make sure the infant's diet is adequate and normal growth patterns are present. Lack of hunger from the infant for more than twenty four hours is generally symptomatic of some condition which must be diagnosed and treated immediately to prevent dire consequences.

Birthed into the Supernatural

The milk requirements for newborn babes in Christ are no less precise than for natural infants. In fact, intake of the milk of the word establishes the foundation upon which the infant's spiritual life will be based. To get this foundation wrong will not only create an inaccurate platform for the infant to live his daily life in Christ but will also make it nearly impossible for anyone to be able to make corrections to this inaccurate foundation in the person's life.

It is so important to keep rehearsing that when we were born again, we did not merely become *"...members..."* of a church as an organization, we were *"...birthed..."* into the kingdom of God. We became an organic part of a living organism, the body of Christ. Becoming members of a church as an organization does not alter a person's existential nature. However, being born again causes a person's existential nature to be radically changed.

I know a young athlete who tore his ACL and became the recipient of ligament transplantation by *"...allograft..."*. This procedure takes ligaments from a cadaver and transplants them into a living being. The cadaver tissue was *"...dead..."* of course, but when sown into the young man's knee, it became a part of his living body. When we were *"...born again..."*, we were baptized into Christ and became a part of His living body. The life of Jesus became our life.

Jesus used a different illustration from the natural world but containing the same type of revelation.

Birthed into the Kingdom

> *"Abide in Me, and I in you. As the branch cannot bear fruit of itself, unless it abides in the vine, neither can you, unless you abide in me. I am the vine, you are the branches. He who abides in Me, and I in him, bears much fruit; for without Me you can do nothing. If anyone does not abide in Me, he is cast out as a branch and is withered; and they gather them and throw them into the fire, and they are burned."* **John 15:1-6**

It is easy to see how the life of the branch is dependent on *"...abiding in the vine..."*. If you remove a branch from the vine, that branch will wither and die. We could even call this a botanical law: The life of any plant is in the vine and then the branches. If any branch loses connection with the vine, it will lose access to its life source, wither, and die. Jesus is endeavoring to get us to see the importance of remaining connected with Him as our life source.

When we were born again, we partook of a new quality of life. Although this new life was spiritual in existence, it was nevertheless new life, and it became ours. If we see ourselves merely as a member of a church as an organization, that sight will establish an incorrect basis for relationship with Christ and with the other members of His body.

It is the will of God that we grow in the knowledge of Him. This knowledge is not meant to be just knowledge about Him but, rather, lead us to develop intimate relationship with Him. Everyone birthed into the kingdom of God is designed to grow in their relationship with God! This relationship is the source of our life!

Birthed into the Supernatural

Everyone who is born again is birthed into the kingdom of God and becomes a part of the living body of Christ. In order to sustain and develop that life, certain requirements must be met. Man does not establish these requirements; God does. Using Jesus' illustration we must abide in the vine in order to sustain the life we have been given and to grow. Using Peter's illustration *"...as newborn babes..."* we must *"...desire the pure milk of the word, that you may grow thereby...".*

Just like prolonged loss of hunger in a natural infant is generally symptomatic of some condition which must be diagnosed and treated immediately to prevent dire consequences so, too, it is for the spiritual infant. Prolonged loss of hunger for the pure milk of the word in a babe in Christ is generally symptomatic of some condition which needs to be diagnosed and treated immediately to prevent dire consequences. Prolonged loss of hunger for the word of God at any stage of a person's spiritual development must be diagnosed and treated. When we were birthed into the kingdom of God, we became spiritual beings requiring the same type of care as people birthed into the natural world. Understanding that we were *"...birthed..."* into the kingdom of God has great bearing on the lives we live in Christ.

Chapter Three

Growth in the Kingdom

Parallel to natural child growth, spiritual children are designed to grow, too. Natural children grow in a very specific manner. The natural body requires a balanced diet comprised of the six major classes of nutrients, carbohydrates, fats, minerals, protein, vitamins, and water, in order to maximize health, energy, and growth. A diversity of foods are required to obtain these nutrients. Digestive fluids within the child's body break down the foods of which the child partakes into usable nutrients necessary to *"...feed..."* the cells of the body causing them to be sustained and to *"...grow..."*.

A spiritual child grows in a very similar fashion. A born again believer's spirit requires spiritual food in order to be nourished. This food is the *"...word of God..."* received either by hearing, reading, or seeing. The word of God must undergo transformation in order to produce the desired results. When a believer receives the word of God, he is receiving knowledge *"...about..."* God. This knowledge must be transformed into actually knowing God or having relationship with God. An illustration from the natural world will provide great understanding here.

When a person receives information about another person in written, audio, or video format, that information does not equate to relationship with the person about whom you have read, heard, or seen. The whole world knew "...*about*..." Nelson Mandela through various formats from news agencies. However, the knowledge we had about Mr. Mandela did not equate to knowing him or having relationship with him.

Just because we read about Peyton Manning and watch him play football on television, the information we receive is just information about him. That information does not mean we know him or have relationship with him. In exactly the same way the information we receive about God through written, audio, or video channels does not equate to knowing Him or having relationship with Him. We receive the information simply as information about God. This information must undergo transformation in order for us to actually know Him or have relationship with Him.

We have already seen a comparable process required in the natural world when a person eats a food item. The digestive fluids of the body break down that food, extracting the usable nutrients contained within it to feed the cells of the body. In a healthy natural body this process functions automatically because that is the way the body was designed.

In the believer, knowledge about God undergoes transformation through the ministry of the Holy Spirit. Jesus told His disciples *"...when He, the Spirit of Truth (the Holy Spirit), has come, He will guide you into all truth..." (John 16: 13)*. Previously, in this same dialogue, Jesus had already identified Himself as *"...I am the way, **the truth**, and the life..." (John 14:6)*. The Holy Spirit has been given the responsibility to guide us as believ-

Growth in the Kingdom

ers *"...into all truth (which is Christ)..."*. However, His ministry does not function automatically. The believer must have his heart turned toward the Lord, desiring to know the Lord, in order for the ministry of the Holy Spirit to transform the word he has received into knowing the Lord or having relationship with Him.

The enemy has employed one of his devices to deceive many into believing just knowing Scripture is enough. If there was a Scripture which could have produced life in us, Jesus would not have been required to die as the sacrificial Lamb of God. Knowing Scripture is vitally important for all believers. However, our knowledge of Scripture is not designed to be a substitute for knowing God! Knowing Scripture is just one step in the process leading to relationship with God. Our goal is not knowing *"...about..."* God but, rather, knowing God! This cannot be done just with a knowledge of Scripture alone.

I remember a perfect illustration from many years ago. A young man cut himself and was bleeding profusely. He said, *"Oh, I can't remember the Scripture that stops bleeding."* Another illustration revealing this deception, also from many years ago, came from a person with a financial need. He dropped his Bible on the floor and promptly stood on it declaring, *"I am standing on the word for this need to be met."* Both of these illustrations demonstrate persons endeavoring to make their knowledge of Scriptures, or in one case the Bible itself, be a substitute for relationship with God.

Birthed into the Supernatural

Paul revealed a remarkable understanding concerning this very matter. He wrote about the contrast between the letter of the word and the Spirit of the word. The context can be found in his explanation to the church at Corinth regarding the difference between ministry in the old covenant versus ministry in the new covenant.

> *"Do we begin again to commend ourselves? Or do we need, as some others, epistles of commendation to you or letters of commendation from you? You are our epistle written in our hearts, known and read by all men; clearly you are an epistle of Christ, ministered by us, written not with ink but by the Spirit of the living God, not on tablets of stone but on tablets of flesh, that is, of the heart. And we have such trust through Christ toward God. Not that we are sufficient of ourselves to think of anything as being from ourselves, but **our sufficiency is from God, who also made us sufficient as ministers of the new covenant, not of the letter but of the Spirit; for the letter kills, but the Spirit gives life**...*"
>
> *II Corinthians 3:1-6*

*(Context **II Corinthians 3:1-18**)*

If a person only has knowledge of Scripture, whether living under the old covenant or the new covenant, what he knows can be called the *"...letter of the word..."*. Knowing the letter of the word with the natural mind in the old covenant did not produce the life God intended for people to have. Even if a person is born again in the new covenant, he can still try to make the knowledge about God derived from Scripture with his natural mind be a substitute for knowing God. Our knowledge about God derived from Scripture must undergo trans-

Growth in the Kingdom

formation through the ministry of the Holy Spirit in order to become relationship with God. The life we received at new birth and the subsequent growth of which we are to partake both come from knowing God, not merely knowing about Him!

In the most intimate setting of Jesus' ministry with His eleven closest disciples, He began to commune with His Father in their presence *(John 17:1-26)*. Most of His prayer was in direct reference to those eleven disciples and *"...for those who will believe in Me through their word..." (John 17:20)*, that includes us. In this prayer Jesus said,

> *"Father, the hour has come. Glorify Your Son, that Your Son also may glorify You, as You have given Him authority over all flesh, that He should give eternal life to as many as You have given Him.* **And this is eternal life, that they may know You, the only true God, and Jesus Christ whom You have sent.** *I have glorified You on the earth. I have finished the work which You have given Me to do."* **John 17:1-4**

An extremely important revelation of a mystery of the kingdom is explained in these few verses of Scripture and also a clue to a second mystery is given. The explanation of the first mystery is a clear and direct statement providing understanding about *"...eternal life...".* Jesus said,

> *Eternal life is knowing God!*

Birthed into the Supernatural

The clue to the second mystery comes in two parts. The first part is the revelation from Jesus who said He was *"...given authority over all flesh, that He should give eternal life to as many as You (the Father) had given Him (the Son)..."*. The second part, also from Jesus saying, *"...I have finished the work which You have given Me to do..."*. These clues open the door to a vital question which must be answered in order to understand the second mystery. **How did Jesus give eternal life to as many as the Father had given Him?**

Because eternal life is *"...knowing God..."*, we can ask our question another way: **How did Jesus create opportunity for people to know God?** The answer can be found in this same intimate context Jesus had with His eleven closest disciples *(This entire intimate context spreads over several chapters of John's Gospel, chapters 14, 15, 16, and 17)*. In the *fourteenth chapter of John* Jesus told His disciples He was going away to prepare a place for them, and they both knew the place and the way to that place *(John 14:1-4)*. *"Thomas said to Him, 'Lord, we do not know where You are going, and how can we know the way?'..." (John 14:5)*. Jesus' response provides us with a very simple answer to our question regarding how He had given eternal life to people by creating opportunity for people to know God.

> *"Jesus said to him (Thomas), 'I am the way, the truth, and the life. No one comes to the Father except through Me. If you had known Me, you would have known My Father also; and from now on you know Him and have seen Him.' Philip said to Him, 'Lord, show us the Father, and it is sufficient for us.' Jesus said to him, 'Have I been with you so long, and yet you have not known Me, Philip?* **He who has seen Me has seen the Father;** *so*

Growth in the Kingdom

how can you say, 'Show us the Father'? Do you not believe that I am in the Father, and the Father in Me? The words that I speak to you I do not speak on My own authority; but the Father who dwells in Me does the works. Believe Me that I am in the Father and the Father in Me, or else believe Me for the sake of the works themselves." ***John 14:6-11***

Because eternal life is *"...knowing God..."*, Jesus gave people opportunity to know God by being One with the Father in such a manner that He could say to His disciples, *"...He who has seen Me has seen the Father..."*. Jesus was not just providing people with academic information *"...about..."* God; He was *"...revealing God..."*! Jesus gave opportunity for people to know God as He *"...knew..."* Him. Jesus offered to introduce people to God with whom He had *"...relationship..."*. According to Jesus' words to His disciples, His ministry was able to be fulfilled as a direct result *"...of His knowing His Father..."*, *"...of His relationship with His Father..." (John 14:6-11)*.

A long time ago I had opportunity to counsel a young woman who had been radically saved, born again right off the streets of a large city. Seeing people saved was very important to her, so she took a course on evangelism. She came into my office one day and burst into tears. As she finally calmed down, I asked her what was wrong. Her reply was so startling it took my breath away.

She gave me a brief testimony of her salvation experience. She explained how very much she loved the Lord Jesus, although no explanation was necessary. Even through her angst and tears she exuded Christ! She said that from the day she

Birthed into the Supernatural

had been saved until recently, she had led at least one person to the Lord every single day. Then she began to weep again. When she could finally speak, she told me about the results from her course on evangelism.

She said since the time she completed her course until then, she had not led one person to the Lord. Before I could ask her any questions, she continued, *"I cannot remember the scriptures nor the order in which they are to be given. I cannot remember what to say."* Through her sobs and tears she asked, *"Is there something wrong with me? Have I lost my salvation?"*

She had not lost her salvation; she had lost understanding of the basis for her salvation: **Relationship with Jesus!** Prior to her course on evangelism, she was introducing people to Jesus, the One who had literally saved her life, the One with whom she had a deep loving relationship. Upon completion of her course, she reduced her *"...living..."* relationship with the *"...living..."* Christ to a series of Scripture references and scripted dialogue.

I am confident whoever had taught this course had not intended this result. I am certain the Scripture references and scripted dialogue had been given merely as tools designed to help a person lead others to the Lord. However, it is not up to the hearers of the word to determine its use and meaning. Ministers have been given the responsibility to *"...steward..."* the word they minister. This young woman's situation demonstrates how easily the devices of the enemy can work against us if we do not keep the difference between the letter of the word and the spirit of the word constantly before us. The results of this young woman's crisis effectively illustrate the understanding about which Paul wrote to the church at Corinth *"...the letter kills, but the Spirit gives life..." (II Corinthians 3:1-6)*.

Another similar illustration, but on the corporate level, also serves to promote understanding regarding the letter of the word. My ministry has primarily been to national Christian leaders in the church living in foreign nations. We typically conduct seminars during the day and crusades in the evening to demonstrate what we have taught during the day. While ministering in a foreign land once, during the evening crusade conducted in a building owned by a local assembly in the area, with several thousand people present, it was my turn to minister the word. At the conclusion of the ministry of the word, I gave an altar call inviting people to receive Jesus. There was a still silence that spread over the hearers, perhaps typical for such an altar call, but no one responded. Then a strange thing happened.

The national Christian leader who oversaw the local assembly in whose building we were conducting the crusade jumped to his feet and came hurriedly to the pulpit speaking in the tongue of the people present. My interpreter interpreted his words for me. *"Whew!"*, he said, *"I was afraid someone would come forward and it would look like we were not doing our job."* This minister's actions demonstrate the same device of the enemy as in the previous illustration regarding the young woman who had been born again from the streets of a large city. The enemy's device had effectively reduced the Spirit of evangelism to the letter of evangelism.

Birthed into the Supernatural

The letter of the word of evangelism reduces the ministry of evangelism to quoting Scripture references, scripted dialogue, and checking a list to make sure we are doing our job. The Spirit of evangelism is all about introducing the lost people of the world who are living without hope to Jesus as the means of their being saved! The letter of the word of evangelism can only exist among people who either do not understand what it means to be born again or who have lost their understanding.

The enemy is relentlessly looking for ways to employ one of his devices to stop the power of the gospel from producing the will of God on the earth. Everything within the church revolves around accurate knowledge of and intimate relationship with our God. *Eternal life is knowing God!* The more we grow in knowing our God, the more we will want to make Him known. Understanding the difference between the letter of the word versus the Spirit of the word and between knowing about God versus knowing God will help us avoid the devices of the enemy.

> *Growth in the kingdom*
> *is growing in the knowledge of God*
> *leading to relationship with God!*

"The people who know their God shall be strong, and carry out great exploits." ***Daniel 11:32***

Chapter Four

Living Like Jesus

Toward the end of Jesus' earthly ministry He began to prepare His eleven closest disciples for His departure. Contained within the context of His time with them, He spoke some of His most remarkable words. These words were recorded by John in *John 14:6-11*. What He said revealed such a profound connection between Him and His Father; His words defy imagination. Jesus said, *"...he who has seen Me has seen the Father..." (John 14:9)*.

Was this intimacy only available to Jesus because He was the Son of God? Was Jesus simply referring to His position as a member of the Trinity? Was this a reflection of a divine attribute only possible for Him as God? Or was this condition the result of a relationship He *"...developed..."* with His Father? We need answers to these questions. Jesus is the pattern for our lives *(I John 2:6)*. We cannot hope to live like Him, nor be *"...expected..."* to live like Him, if we do not know how He lived as He did!

We begin to find answers to our questions by considering the manner in which Jesus came into the world. John wrote about God the Word's existence before He became Jesus the man in ***The Gospel According to John***.

"In the beginning was the Word, and the Word was with God, and the Word was God. He was in the beginning

with God. All things were made through Him, and without Him nothing was made that was made. In Him was life, and the life was the light of men. And the light shines in the darkness, and the darkness did not comprehend it. There was a man sent from God, whose name was John. This man came for a witness, to bear witness of the Light, that all through him might believe. He was not that Light, but was sent to bear witness of that Light. That was the true Light which gives light to every man coming into the world. He was in the world, and the world was made through Him, and the world did not know Him. He came to His own, and His own did not receive Him. But as many as received Him, to them He gave the right to become the children of God, to those who believe in His name; who were born, not of blood, nor of the will of the flesh, nor of the will of man, but of God. **And the Word became flesh and dwelt among us, and we beheld His glory, the glory as of the only begotten of the Father, full of grace and truth.** *John bore witness of Him and cried out, saying, 'This was He of whom I said, 'He who comes after me is preferred before me, for He was before me.' And of His fullness we have all received, and grace for grace. For the law was given through Moses, but* **grace and truth came through Jesus Christ.** **No one has seen God at any time, The only begotten Son, who is in the bosom of the Father, He has declared Him."** *John 1:1-18*

Contained within these eighteen verses is revelation presented in an extremely abbreviated manner regarding the transition of God the Word into Jesus the man.

We know God the Word was clothed in flesh to become Jesus the man through the virgin birth. Jesus did not stop being God just because He was clothed in flesh. Whatever kind of seed you plant, that is what is going to be pro-

Living like Jesus

duced. God's seed was planted in the virgin Mary, and God was produced. Jesus was both God and man. This is a mystery!

However, we gain insights into this mystery through the procreation process of man which presents us with a natural world parallel. A man and a woman conceive a child who becomes both the man and the woman combined in one person. Except for the exclusion of a man in the immaculate conception of the virgin Mary, Jesus went through all the stages required for anyone to be birthed into the natural world, including all of the parts of Mary's pregnancy and delivery.

Jesus lived inside Mary's womb for the same length of time as any other baby would have. He passed through the birthing canal as would have any other child. He needed to have the umbilical cord cut as any other newborn would have. Jesus was birthed into the kingdom of man partaking of flesh and blood as all other men except, of course, for the manner of His conception in a virgin.

> *"Inasmuch then as the children have partaken of flesh and blood, He Himself likewise shared in the same, that through death He might destroy him who had the power of death, that is, the devil, and release those who through fear of death were all their lifetime subject to bondage. For indeed He does not give aid to angels, but He does give aid to the Seed of Abraham. Therefore, in all things He had to be made like His brethren, that He might be a merciful and faithful High Priest in things pertaining to God, to make propitiation for the sins of the people. For in that He Himself has suffered, being tempted, He is able to aid those who are tempted."*
> ***Hebrews 2:14-18***

Birthed into the Supernatural

The letter to the Hebrew Christians gives us a wonderful understanding of one of the reasons for the virgin birth.

> *"For the law, having a shadow of the good things to come, and not the very image of the things, can never with these same sacrifices, which they offer continually year by year, make those who approach perfect. For then would they not have ceased to be offered? For the worshipers, once purified, would have had no more consciousness of sins. But in those sacrifices there is a reminder of sins every year. For it is not possible that the blood of bulls and goats could take away sins. Therefore, when He came into the world, He said:*
>
> *'Sacrifice and offering You did not desire, **but a body You have prepared for Me**. In burnt offerings and sacrifices for sin You had no pleasure. Then I said, 'Behold, I have come -- In the volume of the book it is written of Me -- To do Your will, O God'..."* **Hebrews 10:1-7**

The Father prepared a *"...body..."* in which to clothe God the Word so He could come into the world as *"...the man..."* Jesus. As we have already seen in the letter to the Hebrew Christians, this *"...body..."* had a very specific purpose, *"...that through death He might destroy him who had the power of death, that is, the devil..." **(Hebrews 2:14)**.*

Jesus was God while He walked on the earth, but He chose to divest Himself of His divine attributes. Invisibility, immortality, omniscience, omnipotence, and inability to be tempted were all set aside and replaced with characteristics common to man. We have already seen in Paul's letter to the church at Rome why Jesus needed to become a man and to live as a man on the earth *(**Romans 5:10-21**)*.

Living like Jesus

Having partaken of flesh and blood, divesting Himself of His divine attributes, and choosing to live as a man produced a condition in Jesus the understanding of which is so powerful it will change the way we see Him and ultimately ourselves, forever. John recorded Jesus' words giving us perhaps the simplest and shortest route to accurate understanding in this matter.

*"...Most assuredly, I say to you, **the Son can do nothing of Himself**, but what He sees the Father do; for whatever He does, the Son also does in like manner..."*
John 5:19

Jesus was speaking of Himself here. He was saying He did not fulfill His earthly ministry in His own power as God. Even though He was God and God the Father's Son, He chose to live as a man and could *"...do **nothing** of Himself..."*!

Then how did He fulfill His earthly ministry? How did He do the supernaturally mighty works He did? How did He live such a remarkable life while living in the kingdom of men? Although there are several key factors found in Scripture regarding how He lived the life He lived on earth, the single most important factor was what Jesus Himself emphasized in His declaration to His disciples recorded by John.

"Jesus said to him (Thomas), 'I am the way, the truth, and the life. No one comes to the Father except through Me. If you had known Me, you would have known My Father also; and from now on you know Him and have seen Him.' Philip said to Him, 'Lord, show us the Father, and it is sufficient for us.' Jesus said to him, 'Have I been with you so long, and yet you have not known Me, Philip? He who has seen Me has seen the Father; so

> how can you say, 'Show us the Father'? **Do you not believe that I am in the Father, and the Father in Me? The words that I speak to you I do not speak on My own authority; but the Father who dwells in Me does the works. Believe Me that I am in the Father and the Father in Me, or else believe Me for the sake of the works themselves."** John 14:6-11

In this most holy time with His eleven closest disciples, Jesus revealed the foundational basis for the life and ministry He lived as a man while on earth. Because Jesus had already told them *"...the Son can do **nothing** of Himself..."*, He was now telling them *"...how..."* He was able to fulfill His ministry: **By being one with His Father! Remarkable!**

Why is this significant to "...us..."? This revelation as truth concerning Jesus is astonishing enough, but when you consider Jesus' words immediately following the giving of this revelation, it takes on an overwhelming significance for all who believe.

> *"Most assuredly, I say to you, he who believes in Me, the works that I do he will do also; and greater works than these he will do, because I go to My Father. And whatever you ask in My name, that I will do, that the Father may be glorified in the Son. If you ask anything in My name, I will do it."* **John 14:12-14**

According to revelation contained in Paul's letter to the church at Rome, the means to be born again is believing in Jesus *(Romans 10:13-17)*. Every person who is born again can only be born again by believing in Jesus. According to Jesus, *"...he who believes in Me, will do the works that I do also..."*. **Believers will do the works Jesus did!**

Living like Jesus

It is easy to read verse twelve in a manner which leads to an inaccurate conclusion. It is possible to read this verse to mean if you believe in Jesus, you will do the works He did *"...simply by believing you can do them..."*. In other words, your faith *"...to do the works Jesus did..."* is what makes you able to do them. Is this what Jesus was saying? Is the priority of our faith doing supernatural works? Is that why we have been given faith, to do supernaturally mighty works?

I remember in the early days of ministry failing at certain ministry tasks. Sometimes I would weep because I failed. Other times I would grow frustrated, feeling inadequate, thinking I was just not *"...man enough..."* to walk by faith. I know now the source of the majority of those *"...feelings..."* or *"...thoughts..."* was the enemy. They needed to have been cast down *(II Corinthians 10:3-5)*. The problem was I did not have accurate knowledge of God regarding proper application of my faith. Faith *"...is..."* required as a part of the process of doing supernaturally mighty works; the works are just not the priority of our faith. **Then what is the *"...priority..."* of our faith?**

In order to accurately answer this question we need to look to Jesus as the *"...author and finisher of our faith..." (Hebrews 12:2)*. We have already seen the staggering revelation Jesus gave the Jews regarding His earthly ministry: *"...the Son can do nothing of Himself..." (John 5:19)*. And we have also already seen how Jesus was able to fulfill His earthly ministry:

Birthed into the Supernatural

> *"Jesus was able to live as He lived and do what He did as a direct result of His intimate relationship with His Father!"*

Jesus' entire life and ministry while living as a man on the earth was only possible through His relationship with His Father. It was Jesus Himself who declared that *"...eternal life is knowing God..." (John 17:3)*. Jesus knew His Father, the only true God. That knowledge was the source of His life producing the results of the life He lived.

The desire of our God is for us to be redeemed from the power of darkness and to be translated into the kingdom of His dear Son. Inside that kingdom part of His sovereign plan is to make us flesh and bone parts of His dear Son's body. He has already revealed to us that Jesus as the last Adam *(I Corinthians 15:45-47)* was sent to restore what the first Adam lost *(Romans 5:14,18,19)*. What Adam lost was not primarily dominion and possessions; *it was intimate relationship with God!* It was out of intimacy with God the first Adam had been designed to have dominion and possessions. Jesus, as the last Adam, doing all of God's will was a result of His intimacy with His Father.

The priority of our faith is intimate relationship with our God! Jesus did the supernaturally mighty works that He did as a result of being in the Father and the Father in Him. Jesus gave us an even deeper understanding of this connection regarding the doing of the supernaturally mighty works.

Living like Jesus

*"...Do you not believe that I am in the Father, and the Father in Me? The words that I speak to you I do not speak on My own authority; but **the Father who dwells in Me does the works...**" John 14:10*

Jesus said *"...the Father who dwells in Me does the works..."*. Jesus also said *"...he who believes in Me, the works that I do he will do also..."*. But how will believers be able to do those works?

> ***Believers will be able to do the works Jesus did the same way He did them!***

Jesus lived the life He lived and did the works He did by living in the Father and the Father living in Him. We will live like Jesus lived and do the works Jesus did by living in Christ and having the Christ live in us. Intimate relationship with the Christ is the priority of our faith, *"...not doing supernaturally mighty works..."!* Supernaturally mighty works will be *"...by-products..."* of our relationship with Christ Jesus!

> ***Intimate relationship with Christ is the source of the lives believers are to live and of the works we will do!***

Included in the works believers will do are very specific works about which Matthew was inspired to write regarding the Son of Man judging the nations *(Matthew 25:31-46)*.

Birthed into the Supernatural

"The Son of Man will sit on the throne of His glory and all the nations will be gathered before Him. He will separate them one from another, as a shepherd divides his sheep from the goats. And He will set the sheep on His right hand, but the goats on the left. Then the King will say to those on His right hand, 'Come, you blessed of My Father, inherit the kingdom prepared for you from the foundation of the world: For I was hungry and you gave me food; I was thirsty and you gave Me drink; I was a stranger and you took Me in; I was naked and you clothed Me; I was in prison and you came to Me. Then the righteous will answer Him, saying, Lord, when did we see You hungry and feed You, or thirsty and give You drink? When did we see You a stranger and take You in, or naked and clothe You? Or when did we see You sick or in prison, and come to You? And the King will answer and say to them, 'Assuredly, I say to you, inasmuch as you did it to one of the least of these My brethren, you did it to Me.'..." ***(Matthew 25:37-39).***

The Lord's reasons for the sheep inheriting the kingdom and the sheep's response to those reasons illustrate a very important understanding: What the sheep *"...did..."* to inherit the kingdom was not a result of obedience to commandments the Lord had given them.

Instead, the sheep *"...fed the hungry, gave drink to the thirsty, took in the stranger, clothed the naked, and visited those in prison..."* out of the abundance of their heart. These things done out of the abundance of the heart were the reasons Jesus gave for the sheep inheriting the kingdom. How did their heart become abundantly full of desire to do these things? Some kind of *"...transformation..."* had to have taken place inside of the believers. **But what kind, when, and how?**

Chapter Five
Transformation

We have already stated *(Chapter Three)*, *"Being "...born again..." is as supernatural an event as Mary's virgin conception. It is extremely important for us to understand that when we were born again, we were "...birthed..." into the kingdom of God. This birthing process actually made us children of God. God became our Father as surely as our earthly fathers are our fathers (John 1:11-13)."* The moment a person is born again, they are birthed into the kingdom of God. They are just as much a child of God at the beginning of their new birth as was Paul at the end of his glorious Christian life.

However, we have also already seen that every person who is born again is birthed into the kingdom of God as an infant in need of growth to reach spiritual maturity. This growth is growing in the knowledge of our God as the means of developing relationship with God. The enemy is terrified at the prospects of spiritual growth in the sons of God since knowing God is the source of supernatural life and works. He uses every device imaginable to stop or misdirect our efforts toward spiritual growth. One of his devices producing hideous results is disguised so subtly, it is almost unrecognizable as a device of the enemy.

He tries to deceive believers into accepting their knowledge of Scripture as a *"...substitute..."* for developing relationship with Christ. In many instances, he has taken this

Birthed into the Supernatural

deception to an even deeper level, deceiving Christians into believing their knowledge of Scripture *"...is..."* relationship with the Christ.

Isn't knowing Scripture knowing Jesus? Doesn't Scripture contain knowledge of eternal life so that the more Scripture we know, the more life we have? Excellent questions which need excellent answers either to support the premise that knowledge of Scripture is relationship with Jesus or discover how to develop relationship with Him!

This situation is not new today, nor unique to our generation. Consider one particular incident involving the Jews during Jesus' earthly ministry. Jesus healed a paralytic at the Pool of Bethsaida on the Sabbath. The Jews were enraged that He had done this on the Sabbath causing their persecution of Him to intensify, even desiring to kill Him. To make matters worse, Jesus said *"...My Father has been working until now, and I have been working..." (John 5:17)*. What happened next is of such importance to our understanding the entire Scriptural context needs quoting.

> *"Therefore the Jews sought all the more to kill Him, because He not only broke the Sabbath, but also said that God was His Father, making Himself equal with God.* Then Jesus answered and said to them, "Most assuredly, I say to you, the Son can do nothing of Himself, but what He sees the Father do; for whatever He does, the Son also does in like manner. For the Father loves the Son, and shows Him all things that He Himself does; and He will show Him greater works than these, that you may marvel. For as the Father raises the dead and gives life to them, even so the Son gives life to whom He

Transformation

*will. For the Father judges no one, but has committed all judgment to the Son, that all should honor the Son just as they honor the Father. He who does not honor the Son does not honor the Father who sent Him. Most assuredly I say to you, he who hears My word and believes in Him who sent Me has everlasting life, and shall not come into judgment, but has passed from death into life. Most assuredly, I say to you, the hour is coming, and now is, when the dead will hear the voice of the Son of God; and those who hear will live. For as the Father has life in Himself, so He has granted the Son to have life in Himself, and has given Him authority to execute judgment also, because He is the Son of Man. Do not marvel at this; for the hour is coming in which all who are in the graves will hear His voice and come forth -- those who have done good, to the resurrection of life, and those who have done evil to the resurrection of condemnation. I can of Myself do nothing. As I hear, I judge; and My judgment is righteous, because I do not seek My own will but the will of the Father who sent Me. If I bear witness of Myself, My witness is not true. There is another who bears witness of Me, and I know that the witness which He witnesses of Me is true. You have sent to John, and he has borne witness to the truth. Yet I do not receive testimony from man, but I say these things that you may be saved. He was the burning and shining lamp, and you were willing for a time to rejoice in his light. But I have a greater witness than John's; for the works which the Father has given Me to finish -- the very works that I do -- bear witness of Me, that the Father has sent Me. And the Father Himself, who sent Me has testified of Me. You have neither heard His voice at any time, nor seen His form. But **you do not have His word abiding in you, because whom He sent, Him you do not believe. You search the Scriptures, for in them you think you have eternal life; and these are they which testify of Me. But you are not willing to come to Me that you may have life...**" John 5:17-40*

Birthed into the Supernatural

Even though Jesus' words to these Jews were to persons living under the old covenant, they apply to us, too. The Scriptures, although inspired by God the Holy Spirit, were not given as the means of producing eternal life in us. *"...You search the Scriptures, for in them you think you have eternal life; and these are they which testify of Me. But you are not willing to come to Me that you may have life..."* **John 5:39,40.**

If there could have been a Scripture given to produce eternal life in us, then Jesus would not have had to die! But Jesus did die in order to provide us with the means to obtain eternal life available to us as we *"...come to Him..." (John 5:39,40)!* A person cannot obtain this life only knowing *"...about..."* Jesus. A person must actually know the Lord and enter into a personal relationship with Him as Lord!

The moment we believed in Him and entered into relationship with Him as Lord, a *"...transformation..."* process began in our lives: *"...We were born again...".* After new birth as we grow in the knowledge of Him, *"...transformation..."* continues resulting from the process of renewing our minds.

> *"Do not be conformed to this world, but be **transformed** (3339) by the renewing of your mind..."* **Romans 12:2**
>
> *3339 metamorphoo* from *3326* and *3445*; to *transform* (lit. or fig. "metamorphose"): -- change, transfigure, transform.
>
> ***Strong's Exhaustive Concordance of the Bible***

> **Metamorphoo**, to change into another form. The term is used in reference to believers, **Romans 12:2**, *"...be ye*

Transformation

transformed...", the obligation being to undergo a complete change which, under the power of God, will find expression in character and conduct *(...stress placed on the inward change...)* ...the term is used in ***II Corinthians 3:18*** describing believers as being *"transformed into the same image" (i.e., of Christ in all His moral excellencies)*, the change being effected by the Holy Spirit.

Expository Dictionary of New Testament Words
by W.E. Vine

metamorphose - to change from one form into another; to transform; to subject to or undergo metamorphosis.

metamorphosis - a marked or complete change of character, appearance, condition, etc.

Webster's New Universal Unabridged Dictionary

Transformation cannot be accomplished in a believer as a result of just study, doing good works, or trying harder. The transformation of which Paul wrote *(Romans 12:2)* is only possible in a believer by the power of God. This power works in our lives according to the way of the Lord.

In the second letter to the church at Corinth, Paul began to compare the way of the Lord regarding ministry of the old covenant with ministry of the new covenant. He wrote about Moses covering his face after giving the children of Israel the commandments he had received on Mt. Sinai *(II Corinthians 3:13 originally found in Exodus 34:29-35)*. Paul elaborated about old covenant veils, then transitioned to the concept of veils in the new covenant.

Birthed into the Supernatural

> *"Therefore, since we have such hope, we use great boldness of speech -- unlike Moses, who put a veil over his face so that the children of Israel could not look steadily at the end of what was passing away. But their minds were blinded. For until this day the same veil remains unlifted in the reading of the Old Testament, because the veil is taken away in Christ. But even to this day, when Moses is read, a veil lies on their heart. Nevertheless when one turns to the Lord, the veil is taken away. Now the Lord is the Spirit; and where the Spirit of the Lord is, there is liberty. But we all, with unveiled face, beholding as in a mirror the glory of the Lord, are being transformed into the same image from glory to glory, just as by the Spirit of the Lord."*
> **II Corinthians 3:12-18**

Moses initially placed a veil over his *"...face..."*. However, today when Moses is read, the veil is on the hearers' *"...heart..."*. Paul further writes, *"...the veil is taken away in Christ..."* **(II Corinthians 3:14)**. Then he explains, *"...when one turns to the Lord, the veil is taken away..."*, so the person will be able to behold the glory of the Lord **(II Corinthians 3:16)**. Then he wrote one of the most powerful revelations in the entire New Testament...

> *"...we all, with unveiled face, beholding as in a mirror the glory of the Lord are transformed (3339) into the same image from glory to glory, just as by the Spirit of the Lord..."* **II Corinthians 3:18**

The way of the Lord in order for us to undergo transformation by the power of the Spirit of the Lord is for us to be born again, desire to see *("...or know or have relationship with...")* the Lord, and have our hearts turned toward the Lord. When these conditions are met, any veil will be *"...taken*

Transformation

away...", and we will *"...behold the glory of the Lord...".* The Holy Spirit will most certainly cause us to be transformed under these conditions into the same image as the glory we behold. This is the will and way of the Lord!

The initial transformation for all of us, being born again, provides us with a simple understanding to see how the *"...transformation..."* process is made practical. Anyone can be saved...

> *"...If you confess with your mouth the Lord Jesus and believe in your heart that God has raised Him from the dead, you will be saved..."* **Romans 10:9-10**

> *"...For whoever calls on the name of the Lord shall be saved. How then shall they call on Him in whom they have not believed? And how shall they believe in Him of whom they have not heard? And how shall they hear without a preacher? And how shall they preach unless they are sent?..."* **Romans 10:13,14**

Scripture is showing us prerequisites required prior to our believing **(Romans 14:14,15)**. We must first *"...hear..."* of Jesus. Scripture also makes it clear not everyone who hears is going to receive Jesus nor believe in Him.

> *"He (Jesus) came to His own, and His own did **not** receive Him. But as many as received Him, to them He gave the right (authority) to become children of God, to those who believe in His name: who were born, not of blood, nor of the will of the flesh, nor of the will of man, but of God." ***John 1:11-13**

Even a person who does *"...receive..."* Jesus **(John 1:12)** needs other provisions required from God in order to complete their salvation process. Scripture is very specific regarding God's provisions in order to be saved.

> *"For by grace you have been saved through faith, and that not of yourselves; it is the gift of God, not of works, lest anyone should boast."* **Ephesians 2:8**

> *"...no one can say that Jesus is Lord except by the Holy Spirit..."* **I Corinthians 12:3**

After a person *"...preaches..."* in order for the hearers to be saved, they must accept that Jesus born of a virgin as the sinless Lamb of God to take away the sin of the world was crucified dead and buried, rose again on the third day, and has become Lord. If the hearers *"...receive..."* the truth about Jesus as preached and desire to enter into relationship with Him, three things happen:

1. The Lord grants them *"...right (authority)..." (John 1:12)* to become children of God.

2. This *"...right..."* releases God's provision for the Holy Spirit to *"...reveal..."* Jesus as Lord in order for them to be able to enter into relationship with Him as Lord.

3. This *"...right..."* also releases God's provision for the hearers to partake of *"...faith..."* from God as the supernaturally endowed ability necessary for them to be able to *"...believe..."* in Jesus.

The immaculate conception *"...required..."* the involvement of God, His will, and His power. Mary's actions were in direct response to the revealed will of God known by her. Her

Transformation

willingness to participate in God's will released His power to bring about His will in her life.

New birth, too, can only happen in direct response to the revealed will of God *("...how shall they believe in Him of whom they have not heard..." **Romans 10:14**)*. Our willingness to participate in God's will is what releases His power necessary for us to be born again *("...as many as received Him, to them He gave the right (authority) to become children of God..." **John 1:12**)*. Being born again is as supernatural as was the immaculate conception.

Having access to the supernatural provisions of God required to complete our new birth process revolves around our willingness to participate in the revealed will of God for us specifically, just like Mary's pregnancy. God's will does not manifest in our lives simply because He wills it. We must be willing participants to His revealed will as it is made known to us.

The *"...transformations..."* we seek will only happen if the veils are removed so we can behold the glory of the Lord. The veils will be removed *"...if..."* we turn our heart toward the Lord desiring to see *("...or know, or have relationship with...")* Him according to His will. *God wills for us to be transformed. However,...*

Our transformation requires our willing participation!

Birthed into the Supernatural

New birth gave us a simple understanding of how the *"...transformation..."* process is made practical from the perspective of the one being born again. The perspective of the one who goes to *"...preach..."* about Jesus in order for new birth to be possible adds an important component to our understanding.

In **Chapter Three** we considered the young woman who had been radically saved from the streets of a large city. Her zeal for *"...winning the lost..."* inspired her to take a course on evangelism. *"Prior to her course on evangelism, she was introducing people to Jesus, the One who had literally saved her life, the One with whom she had a deep loving relationship. Upon completion of her course, she reduced her "...living..." relationship with the "...living..." Christ to a series of Scripture references and scripted dialogue."*

This young woman desired to see people *"...transformed..."* by the power of God through new birth, just as she had been. Her transformation had been a direct result of entering into relationship with Jesus. She did not just know about the Lord; she knew Him! Her desire was to introduce people to the One whom she knew, who had changed her life, and was the daily source of the life she lived.

If we are ever going to fulfill our roles as ministers of reconciliation, we must change the way we approach evangelism. We must simplify the process by focusing on introducing people to the One who saved us and by whom we live our daily lives: ***Jesus our Lord!***

Chapter Six

Submission to Live

Even the term *"...submission...."* has become repugnant to many in the *"...church world..."*, conjuring up images of control, abuse, or some other malevolent concept. Submission is not an evil from the kingdom of darkness! Submission is a vital component of the kingdom of God!

> *"Submit (5293) to God. Resist the devil and he will flee from you. Draw near to God and He will draw near to you..."* **James 4:7,8**
>
> *5293 hupotasso* from *5259* and *5021*; to *subordinate*; reflex. to *obey*: -- be under obedience (obedient), put under, subdue unto, (be, make) subject (to, unto), be (put) in subjection (to, under), submit self unto.
>
> **Strong's Exhaustive Concordance of the Bible**
>
> **submit** - to yield, resign, or surrender to the power, will, or authority of another or others: often used reflexively.
>
> **Webster's New Universal Unabridged Dictionary**

According to **James 4:7** submission to God is the first step in ridding ourselves of demonic activity. The life every born again person lives in Christ, received at the time of our new birth, is predicated on our submission to Jesus as Lord *(Romans 10:9,10)!*

Birthed into the Supernatural

Jesus was submitted to do the will of His Father, rather than doing His own will, during the entirety of His earthly ministry including death on the cross. Perhaps the most direct references to this fact found in Scripture are the words of Jesus Himself recorded by John and Matthew...

> *"I can of Myself do nothing. As I hear, I judge: and My judgment is righteous, because **I do not seek My own will but the will of the Father who sent Me.**"*
> **John 5:30**

> *"O My Father, if it is possible, let this cup pass from Me; nevertheless, **not as I will, but as You will.**"*
> **Matthew 26:39**

James wrote more about submission than just what we read in **James 4:7**. The words the Holy Spirit inspired him to write are most revealing regarding the comprehensive nature of submission designed for our lives in Christ.

> *"Come now, you who say, 'Today or tomorrow we will go to such and such a city, spend a year there, buy and sell, make a profit'; whereas you do not know what will happen tomorrow. For what is your life? It is even a vapor that appears for a little time and then vanishes away. Instead you ought to say, 'If the Lord wills, we shall live and do this or that.' But now you boast in your arrogance. All such boasting is evil. Therefore, to him who knows to do good and does not do it, to him it is sin."* **James 4:13-17**

Jesus is not asking us to submit to Him so He can have control over us. He is asking us to submit to Him so we can benefit from the authority He has been given as Head of His own body, whose body parts we are!

Submission to Live

When we plunge head long into doing our own will without even considering His will, we eliminate the possibility of reaping the benefits from His authority. James called this arrogance surely because it gives the impression we think we know as much as does the Lord. *We do not!* Or it gives the impression that we do not care what the Lord wills. *Do we?*

If God was only interested in being in control of our lives, He did not have to send His only begotten Son to be born of a virgin, to live as a man, and to die the horrible death of the cross to do so. The Sovereign Omnipotent God is without equal. He could have simply subjugated us! Yet, He did not; He *"...asked..."* for our submission!

Being born again involves our willingness to submit to Jesus as Lord. According to the definition of submission, *"...to yield to the authority of another..."*, in the case of new birth, the authority is Jesus. Why would we yield to the authority of Jesus? Because when we received the truth about Jesus being the source of eternal life, the Holy Spirit revealed Jesus' Lordship to us as the means to this life. We then gladly yielded to His authority as Lord in order to partake of eternal life.

Everything in the kingdom of God depends on the order God has established and submission to that order. Without the order of God operational in His kingdom, chaos will rule. Chaos ruling because the sons of the kingdom are ignorant of the way of God is easily correctable. But if the sons of the kingdom understand the order of God and simply refuse to submit to it, that is anarchy.

Birthed into the Supernatural

anarchy

1. the complete absence of government and law.
2. political disorder and violence; lawlessness.
3. disorder in any sphere of activity.

Webster's *New Universal Unabridged Dictionary*

Jesus will not force us to submit to Him. That would be control. Neither will He punish us if we do not submit to Him. However, if we refuse to submit to Him and instead do what is right in our own eyes, there will be negative consequences. A natural world illustration will serve us well here.

A little child watches from a safe distance as his mother cooks a meal on an electric stove. The child is enamored with the red glow of the stove. His mother sees his fascination with the red glow and tells him not to touch it because it is hot; it will harm him. The child's mother is not trying to control her child; she is trying to help her child avoid a negative consequence. The mother goes to the kitchen sink, only a step away from the stove, to drain the liquid from something she is cooking. The child seizes opportunity and touches the beautiful red glowing stove top.

The child screams in horror for the pain of the burn. Was the child's pain punishment from his mother because he disobeyed her? Did the child's pain bring pleasure to his mother? Did the child's mother gloat over the severity of the consequence? Of course the answer to all of these foolish questions is, *"No!"* However, just because the answer is no,

Submission to Live

the child still suffered a negative consequence from his lack of submission to his mother.

Or maybe a different type of question needs to be asked, "Why did the child's mother allow this to happen?" No matter how protective a parent may be over their child, it is impossible to keep a child from all harm. No matter what precautions a parent may take, a child can still touch a hot surface, run with scissors, cut himself with a sharp instrument, or do some other thing in violation of his parents' will and suffer negative consequences.

The illustration of the child is easy to see and understand. The principle of it works the same way in the kingdom of God. Jesus desires to teach us the way of His kingdom so we may live the lives He died to provide. However, the choice to submit to the way of the Lord is ours. He will not control us! If we refuse to submit to Him, His will, and His way, there will be negative consequences. It is the wrong question to ask why the Lord would allow negative consequences if those consequences result from our choice not to submit to Him. The correct question would be, *"Why would we refuse to submit?"* Our submission creates the greatest opportunity for us to reap the benefit from His Lordship. We submit because we desire to *"...live..."* in the authority of our God.

Now, what does Jesus *"...require..."* of us as sons of the kingdom? The priority of His commandments is to *"...seek first the kingdom of God and His righteousness..." (Matthew 6:33)*. **Ten verses in the sixth chapter of Matthew** of which **verse thirty-three** is a part provide context which contributes to our understanding of the commandments of the Lord *(Matthew 6:25-34)*. Jesus contrasted life oriented to the natural world with life oriented to the spiritual world in these ten verses. He did not command us to avoid desire for anything from the natural world, just *"...not..."* to make desires for natural things our priority.

Of all of the commandments the Lord has given us, the one commandment upon which all others depend is for us to grow in the knowledge of Him *(I Peter 2:2)*. Jesus said, *"...this is eternal life, that they may know You, the only true God, and Jesus Christ whom You have sent..." (John 17:3)*. The entirety of this book is devoted to promoting accurate understanding how eternal life in the kingdom of God comes as a result of knowing God. Whether being born again, growing in the kingdom, living like Jesus, undergoing transformation, loving one another, or obeying the Lord, everything is designed to work as a direct result of being *"...one with God..."*!

As we have already established in **Chapter Four**, *"Jesus lived the life He lived and did the works He did by living in the Father and the Father living in Him. We will live like Jesus lived and do the works Jesus did by living in Christ and having the Christ live in us. Intimate relationship with the Christ is the priority of our faith...".*

This relationship must be *"...developed..."* by abiding in Christ and growing in the knowledge of Him. We have already established, *"...everyone who is born again is birthed into the kingdom of God as an infant in need of growth to reach spiritual maturity...".* If every newborn in Christ would

Submission to Live

submit to this simple understanding, it would be easier to help him learn what it means to *"...abide..."* in Christ and to *"...grow..."* in the knowledge of Him. Every newborn in Christ is to...

> *"...desire the pure milk of the word, that you may grow thereby..."* **I Peter 2:2**

Such submission would help create a life of desire for the word of God as the spiritual food by which we live and grow.

The church at Laodicea was in trouble *(Revelation 3:14-22)* demonstrating loss of successful life and growth from the word of God. Developing relationship with Jesus was no longer their priority. They had become so deceived, they did not *"...know..."* their true condition *(Revelation 3:17)*. While there is no Scriptural record stating exactly what caused the Laodiceans to become so deceived, Scripture does directly address one way believers can be deceived.

> *"Therefore lay aside all filthiness and overflow of wickedness, and receive with meekness the implanted word, which is able to save your souls. But **be doers of the word, and not hearers only, deceiving yourselves**. For if anyone is a hearer of the word and not a doer, he is like a man observing his natural face in a mirror; for he observes himself, goes away, and immediately forgets what kind of man he was..."* **James 1:21-24**

James wrote that being a hearer only and not a doer of the word causes a person to deceive himself. If we apply this revelation to the believers at Laodicea, we can determine their deception was at least in part a result of their not being doers of the word. They either had not maintained their spiritual desire for the word or they had not continued in the word as doers, thereby deceiving themselves, forgetting what manner of men they were.

We need Scripture, the inspired written word of God, which provides us with knowledge about God as seeds we plant within us. However, spiritual growth is a result of knowing God, not just knowing about Him. The seeds we plant from Scripture must undergo transformation by the ministry of the Holy Spirit. His transforming work provides us with a living revelation of God giving us opportunity to know Him.

Spiritual maturity is defined in Scripture as...

"...coming to the unity of the faith and of the knowledge of the Son of God, to a perfect man, to the measure of the stature of the fullness of Christ; that we should no longer be children, tossed to and fro and carried about with every wind of doctrine, by the trickery of men, in the cunning craftiness of deceitful plotting, but, speaking the truth in love, may grow up in all things into Him who is the head -- Christ -- from whom the whole body, joined and knit together by what every joint supplies, according to the effective working by which every part does its share, causes growth of the body for the edifying of itself in love..." **Ephesians 4:13-16**

We have labored carefully to establish understanding of a profoundly important truth, Scripture must *"...never..."* become a substitute for God. *Our lives depend on knowing God!* We accept Scripture as the inspired word of God, and we further accept the tremendously important place it has in our lives. However, if there could have been a Scripture

Submission to Live

given which could have produced eternal life in us, then Jesus would not have had to die.

Scripture is not Christ!

> *"You must continue in the things which you have learned and been assured of, knowing from whom you have learned them, and that from childhood **you have known the Holy Scriptures, which are able to make you wise for salvation through faith which is in Christ Jesus. All Scripture is given by inspiration of God, and is profitable for doctrine, for reproof, for correction, for instruction in righteousness**, that the man of God may be complete, thoroughly equipped for every good work."*
> **II Timothy 3:16,17**

Lack of understanding between Scripture as the inspired word of God and Jesus as the living word of God opens a door for *"...confusion..."* regarding the word. Scripture as the inspired word of God *"...is not..."* Jesus the living word of God.

> *"For the word of God is living and powerful, and sharper than any two-edged sword, piercing even to the division of soul and spirit, and of joints and marrow, and is a discerner of the thoughts and intents of the heart. And there is no creature hidden from His sight, but all things are naked and open to the eyes of Him to whom we must give account."* **Hebrews 4:12,13**

The living word of God is a person! Establishing distinction between the inspired written word of God and the living word of God in no way diminishes the value, authenticity, nor inspiration of Scripture. It is intended to exalt the Christ as the living word of God, allowing Scripture to take its rightful place in our lives, not exalted beyond its purpose *(II Timothy 3:16,17)!*

> ***The priority of our submission must always be to Jesus!***

Once this priority is established in our lives, and only then, will *"...submission to live..."* function according to the design of the Lord.

Chapter Seven

Deception Undetected

The medical community is constantly reminding the members of our society of the importance of *"...early detection..."* for certain diseases. The medical premise is that early detection makes it more efficient to treat the disease. The longer a disease goes undetected, the more associated health risks are made possible. This medical principle can easily be applied to our lives in the kingdom of God. Early detection of a deception makes it easier to deal with the deception. The longer a deception goes undetected, the more difficult it is to remove, and an undetected deception becomes a corrupt environment into which more deceptions can be added.

The enemy desperately desires to steal our identity because knowing who we are in Christ and who Christ is in us is what causes us to walk like Christ. The enemy uses many devices in an effort to fulfill his desire. A believer's true identity poses a terrible threat to the enemy, and because it does, he deploys one of his first devices against those who believe just after new birth. Because a person's spirit is born again rather than their body or their soul, being birthed into the kingdom of God does not require tangible evidence for the body or soul. The enemy uses this condition in an effort to shift the focus of new birth from the spirit to the natural by sowing seeds into the new believer to be concerned about how he looks, feels, or thinks, trying to get the new believer to forsake his

Birthed into the Supernatural

new birth. Whether a person looks or feels or even thinks any differently immediately after being born again does not necessarily negate nor support the believer's new birth.

Spiritual children require monitoring, just like natural children, to create the most suitable environment for the health of the infant. That is, a new believer must have a more mature believer involved with him to help him maintain a spiritual focus. Because we are saved *"...by grace through faith, and that not of yourselves; it is the gift of God..." (Ephesians 2:8)*, the new believer needs help learning to embrace his new birth by *"...faith..."* rather than by sight or feelings!

"For we walk by faith, not by sight." **II Corinthians 5:7**

The enemy's next level of attack is more subtle. If he cannot cause the believer to forsake his new birth, he introduces a new device. This new device includes an element of *"...truth..."* but from a corrupt perspective. He endeavors to convince the new believer his true identity has not really changed, even though *"...saved by grace..." (Ephesians 2:8)*. Remember Jesus said, *"...The thief does not come except to steal, and to kill, and to destroy..." (John 10:10)*.

The enemy's tactics include *"...sayings..."* designed to cause his deception to complete its work, stealing the believer's true identity. These sayings focus on inspiring persons who are saved to believe a lie and then to say what they believe. Anytime you are inspired to say something about yourself using the phrase *"...I am..."*, make sure what you are about to say is based on the truth and not a lie.

Deception Undedected

Look at what Scripture says specifically about the change of our identity after new birth.

> *"Therefore, from now on we regard no one according to the flesh. Even though we have known Christ according to the flesh, yet now we know Him thus no longer. Therefore,* **if anyone is in Christ, he is a new creation; old things have passed away; behold all things have become new...** *He made Him who knew no sin to be sin for us, that we might become the righteousness of God in Him."* **II Corinthians 5:16-21**

> *"Therefore we were buried with Him through baptism into death, that just as Christ was raised from the dead by the glory of the Father, even so we also should walk in newness of life. For if we have been united together in the likeness of His death, certainly we also shall be in the likeness of His resurrection, knowing this,* **that our old man was crucified with Him, that the body of sin might be done away with, that we should no longer be slaves of sin. For he who has died has been freed from sin."** **Romans 6:4-6** *(context* **Romans 5:12-6:23)**

The device used in the enemy's second attack is designed to get the new believer to say *"...I am..." "...a sinner...", "...unworthy...", "...just human...",* anything less than what new birth has transformed him to be. If it is successful, it will deceive the new believer into seeing his current identity in Christ the same as prior to being born again, effectively stealing the results of his new birth. At new birth a person becomes a *"...new creature in Christ..."!*

The verb *"...to be..."* in various applications involving a noun or pronoun is used to identify the state of existence of a person, place, or thing. When used in the present tense, it refers to the current state of existence of the person, place, or thing. For example, He *"...is..."* born again. It *"...is..."* hot at

Birthed into the Supernatural

the beach. New York *"...is..."* a large city. When used in the first person, present tense, it conveys the current state of the person about whom the verb is used. For example, I *"...am..."* born again. The subtle device of the enemy is used to persuade the believer his identity has either not changed or to establish it on the wrong foundation. If the device works, the believer will believe he has not really changed.

For a believer to proclaim, *"...I am..." "...a sinner...", "...unworthy...", "...just human...",* anything less than what new birth has transformed him to be, he is declaring his current state as *"...I am the same as I always have been...".* This is very problematic for the church. We must not rewrite the English language to support inaccurate doctrine. The verb *"...to be..."* when used in the first person present tense identifies the current state of existence of the person using the first person pronoun, *"...I am...".*

Instead of rewriting the English language to support inaccurate doctrine, we must identify the inaccuracy and change it, so it conforms accurately to the will of God. We are responsible to use the words of our language appropriately so the hearers may easily understand our meaning. The hearers are not responsible to ascribe an alternate meaning to words of our language commonly understood one way so we may understand how a person has used those words to mean something else.

"For a good tree does not bear bad fruit, nor does a bad tree bear good fruit. For every tree is known by its own fruit. For men do not gather figs from thorns, nor

Deception Undedected

do they gather grapes from a bramble bush. A good man out of the good treasure of his heart brings forth good; and an evil man out of the evil treasure of his heart brings forth evil..."

> *"...For out of the abundance of the heart his mouth speaks."*
>
> **Luke 6:43-45 & Matthew 12:33-37**

Every time a believer declares, *"...I am..." "...a sinner...", "...unworthy...", "...just human..."*, anything less than what new birth has transformed him to be, according to Scripture *(Luke 6:43-45 & Matthew 12:33-37)*, his declaration comes directly out of the abundance of his heart. Scripture also teaches, *"...as a man thinks in his heart, so is he..." (Proverbs 23:7)*. When we combine *"...out of the abundance of the heart his mouth speaks..."* and *"...as a man thinks in his heart, so is he..."*, we understand a man's words reveal how he thinks about himself in his heart. Every time a person speaks *"...inaccurately..."* about his identity, his words, in agreement with his own heart, help keep his deception in place.

What is our current state of existence? *"...less than what new birth transformed us to be..."* or *"...new creatures in Christ..."*? Are we currently *"...bound by sin..."* or *"...freed from sin..."*? It cannot be both ways at the same time. We must choose one way or the other. Be careful! Whatever you choose is going to determine your future. We must not base our future on a deception which is most certainly based on a lie.

Birthed into the Supernatural

If the enemy's device succeeds and the new believer is deceived to think of himself less than what his new birth actually transformed him to be, this deception will most surely be compounded by other deceptions. Remember, according to Jesus, *...The thief does not come except to steal, and to kill, and to destroy..." (**John 10:10**)*. The enemy desires to steal the identity of all believers.

The next device of the enemy involves uniting the deceived believer with other believers whose identities have also been stolen. If the enemy can successfully steal the identities of individual believers and join them together, he will then target their corporate identity. The enemy does not want the church on the earth to see who we really are: We are the flesh and bone body of Christ Himself! Jesus said, *"...he who believes in Me, the works that I do he will do also..." (**John 14:12**)*. Can you imagine the horror this thought must bring to the enemy, to have many such believers joined together? He understands how important it is to him and his evil kingdom to keep believers from seeing who they really are and to keep us divided!

The enemy has developed perhaps his most insidious device in order to steal our corporate identity. He has launched the lie that the church is simply a place we go. Scripture says, *"...the God of our Lord Jesus Christ, the Father of glory..."* has, *"...put all things under His (Jesus') feet, and gave Him to be head over all things to the church, which is His body, the fullness of Him who fills all in all." (**Ephesians 1:22,23**)*. In this same letter to the church at Ephesus, Paul was inspired to write more on this matter...

Deception Undedected

"...Husbands ought to love their own wives as their own bodies; he who loves his wife loves himself. For no one ever hated his own flesh, but nourishes and cherishes it, just as the Lord does the church. For we are members of His body, of His flesh and of His bones. 'For this reason a man shall leave his father and mother and be joined to his wife, and the two shall become one flesh.' This is a great mystery, but I speak concerning Christ and the church..." **Ephesians 5:28-32**

The life of any body part depends on remaining attached to the body. If a body part is cut off from the body of which it is a part for any reason, it will immediately begin to die. If the enemy's device deceives any of the parts of the body of Christ into believing the church is less than a living organism of which we are living parts, the very life of the parts who are deceived will be in jeopardy. If the church is seen only as a place we go, that means all the times we are not at church we will see the church less than it really is. If we see the church as a place we go, even when we are at church, we will see the church less than it really is. ***We do not go to church; we are the church!*** Here is a profoundly important understanding regarding our identities:

> ***Eternal is greater than temporal!***

"Therefore we do not lose heart. Even though our outward man is perishing, yet the inward man is being renewed day by day. For our light affliction, which is but for a moment, is working for us a far more exceeding and eternal weight of glory, while we do not look at the things which are seen, but at the things which are not

> seen. For the things which are seen are temporal (4340), but the things which are not seen are eternal (166)."
> **II Corinthians 4:16-18**
>
> **4340 proskairos** from *4314* and *2540*; *for the occasion only*, i.e. *temporary*: -- dur- [eth] for awhile, endure for a time, for a season, temporal.
>
> **166 aionios** from *165*; *perpetual* (also used of past time, or past and future as well): -- eternal, forever, everlasting, world (began).

Our spiritual identities are eternal; our natural identities are temporal. Our eternal sonship, *"...born, not of blood, nor of the will of the flesh, nor of the will of man, but of God..." **(John 1:13)**,* has priority over our temporal sonship. The entire kingdom of God is oriented to the eternal. If the enemy can cause us to shift our focus to our natural temporal selves as our priority, he will win. Eternal is greater than temporal. Every aspect of our lives in Christ begins with our sight of spiritual eternal things and moves out of the invisible toward the visible natural temporal. If the enemy can cause us to reverse the process, he will abort the very life we seek!

In one of the most significant verbal exchanges Jesus had with His closest disciples, He asked them, *"...Who do men say that I, the Son of Man, am..." **(Matthew 16:13)***? His disciples gave Him a few answers. Then Jesus asked them, *"...But who do you say that I am?..." **(Matthew 16:15)***. The following exchange between Peter and Jesus defines the foundation of the church.

> "Simon Peter answered and said, 'You are the Christ, the Son of the living God.' Jesus answered and said to

Deception Undedected

him, 'Blessed are you, Simon Bar-Jonah, for flesh and blood has not revealed this to you, but My Father who is in heaven. And I also say to you that you are Peter, and on this rock I will build My church, and the gates of Hades shall not prevail against it..." **Matthew 16:17,18**

Interpretation of this portion of Scripture has provided controversy for centuries regarding the role of the man Peter. Without becoming embroiled in this controversy, we know Peter was an important apostle of the Lord Jesus Christ fulfilling his purpose on earth. We do not wish to take anything away from this godly and important historical figure nor his role of ministry in the church.

However, Scripture also states *"...no other foundation can anyone lay than that which is laid, which is Jesus Christ..." (**I Corinthians 3:11**)*. And most certainly more importantly the church is the body of Christ *(**Ephesians 1:15-23; Ephesians 5:22-33**)!* Jesus told His eleven closest disciples, *"...this is eternal life, that they may know You, the only true God, and Jesus Christ whom You have sent..." (**John 17:3**)*. Knowing the Father, Jesus, and their true identities is what causes us to partake of eternal life and enter into the body of Christ as His flesh and bone body parts.

The enemy knows how important stealing a person's identity can be in promoting his agenda. If the enemy can steal the Father's and Jesus' true identity from us, we cannot be saved. If the enemy can steal our identity after we are *"...saved by grace...",* he will effectively rob us of the benefits of having been born again. Although there are a myriad of deceptions in the enemy's arsenal directed at the church, the one about which we need to be primarily concerned is *"...identity theft..."*. This device serves as trigger to all the rest and will abort our benefits from being born again!

Chapter Eight

Eternal Fundamentals

John the Beloved, inspired by God the Holy Spirit, revealed the will of God regarding the lives of all believers: *"...He who says he abides in Him ought himself also to walk just as He walked."* *(I John 2:6)*. **What an extraordinary revelation!** We have already seen *(Chapter Four)* the supernatural life Jesus lived was not a result of His own power as God *(John 5:19)* but, rather, His intimacy with His Father *(John 14:9-11)*. In order to live as Jesus lived we, too, must have intimate relationship with our God. In order to fulfill God's expectations to develop intimate relationship with Him, there are some fundamentals we must acquire.

The natural world and the spiritual world are two completely separate environments in which different rules govern life in each. There is an illustration from the natural world involving two such completely separate environments: the earth and the sea. Although the sea exists on the earth, it is an exclusive environment from the earth. The creatures which inhabit each of these two environments do so in an exclusive manner. That is, the *"...deer which pants for the water..."* *(Psalms 42:1)* lives on land, only desiring water to drink. The *"...fish of the sea..."* *(Genesis 1:26)* live in the water and cannot live on the land.

Paul wrote about man, considering the difference between the outward man and the inward man. He contrasted these two in a simple, albeit peculiar manner.

Birthed into the Supernatural

> *"...We do not lose heart, even though our outward man is perishing, yet the inward man is being renewed day by day. For our light affliction, which is but for a moment, is working for us a far more exceeding and eternal weight of glory, while we do not look at the things which are seen, but at the things which are not seen. For the things which are seen are temporary, but the things which are not seen are eternal."*
> **II Corinthians 4:16-18**

Because man is spirit, soul, and body all in one person, he represents a type of microcosm of the natural world and the spiritual world. Man is comprised of both natural and spiritual parts. The natural is temporal. The spiritual is eternal. Jesus made it clear to Nicodemus our spirit is what must be born again, not our flesh. Man does not, cannot, enter his mother's womb a second time to be born again. Our outward man, our natural body, which we can see is temporal. Our inward man, our born again spirit, which we cannot see is eternal.

The natural and the spiritual are separate from one another and mutually exclusive. Although the natural world exists within the spiritual world, it is exclusive from it, just like the sea is exclusive from the earth. Although man's spirit abides within his body, it is exclusive from his body, also just like the sea is exclusive from the earth. Man's life in the kingdom of God is oriented to his spirit, not his flesh.

Eternal things *"...**not** seen..."* have precedence over temporal things *"...seen..."*. The temporal things by definition are *"...temporary..."*. Absolutely everything about God

Eternal Fundamentals

and all of the provisions available to mankind through Christ are eternal. This understanding sets the stage for every facet of our lives in Christ. Our eternal spiritual lives are designed to take precedence over our temporal natural lives. ***How does this work?***

Consider salvation as an illustration: ***What is the basis of our redemption?*** Jesus gave Nicodemus a wonderful synopsis of the plan of God to save mankind.

> *"No one has ascended to heaven but He who came down from heaven, that is, the Son of Man who is in heaven. And as Moses lifted up the serpent in the wilderness, even so must the Son of Man be lifted up, that whoever believes in Him should not perish but have eternal life. For God so loved the world that He gave His only begotten Son, that whoever believes in Him should not perish but have everlasting life. For God did not send His Son into the world to condemn the world, but that the world through Him might be saved."* ***John 3:13-17***

Jesus came into the world as *"...the Lamb of God to take away the sin of the world..." (John 1:29)*. He accomplished this by living a sinless life so He could be the sacrifice to take away our sins *(II Corinthians 5:21; I Peter 1:18-21)*. He died on the cross as the ultimate sacrifice, carrying our sins in Himself, allowing His own blood to be shed for us *(I Peter 2:23-25)*. Jesus' death, burial, and resurrection provide salvation for all mankind.

Paul wrote, *"...whoever calls on the name of the Lord shall be saved..." (Romans 10:13)*. Every time a person calls on the name of the Lord, he will be saved. ***Does Jesus have to die over and over again every time anyone calls on Him for salva-***

Birthed into the Supernatural

tion? Scripture teaches *"...Christ, having been raised from the dead, dies no more. Death no longer has dominion over Him. For the death that He died, He died to sin once for all..." (Romans 6:9,10).*

> "For he who has died has been freed from sin. **Now if we died with Christ, we believe that we shall also live with Him, knowing that Christ, having been raised from the dead, dies no more. Death no longer has dominion over Him. For the death that He died, He died to sin once for all**; but the life that He lives, He lives to God..." **Romans 6:7-10**

Jesus does not have to die over and over again every time anyone calls on Him for salvation. He *"...died once for all..."*. Because the basis for our redemption is the foundational revelation for our entire lives in Christ, we need to see it in several Scripture references...

> "...the blood of Jesus Christ His Son cleanses us from all sin..." **I John 1:7**

> "...Christ came as High Priest of the good things to come, with the greater and more perfect tabernacle not made with hands, that is, not of this creation. Not with the blood of goats and calves, but with His own blood He entered the Most Holy Place once for all, having obtained eternal redemption..." **Hebrews 9:11,12**

> "...Therefore, brethren, having boldness to enter the Holiest by the blood of Jesus, by a new and living way which He consecrated for us, through the veil, that is His flesh..." **Hebrews 10:19,20**

The redemption we obtained through Jesus Christ is an *"...eternal redemption..." (Hebrews 9:12).* That is, Jesus' sacrifice as *"...the Lamb of God to take away the sin of the world..." (John*

Eternal Fundamentals

1:29) will last forever! The *"...blood of bulls and goats and the ashes of a heifer..." (Hebrews 9:13)* used as sacrifices for sin in the old covenant are temporal and have to be sacrificed year after year *(Hebrews 10:1)*. Jesus needed to die only once. His blood is eternally alive, cleansing us from all sin, providing eternal redemption for all.

Because the redemption Christ provides is an *"...eternal redemption..." (Hebrews 9:12)*, it is greater than anything temporal. The laws of the natural temporal universe do not apply to anything eternal. Past, present, and future are all temporal terms. Jesus' death, burial, and resurrection are eternal. That is why Jesus does not have to die over and over again every time anyone calls on Him for salvation. The *"...eternal redemption..." (Hebrews 9:12)* He provided is for all mankind for all generations for all time. All man has to do is appropriate what already exists!

How does an unsaved person appropriate this eternal redemption? The natural world exists within the spiritual world like in the illustration of the sea and the earth: They are mutually exclusive but exist together. An unsaved person lives on the earth which exists within the spiritual world, in the same manner a fish lives in the sea which exists on the earth. The *"...eternal redemption..."* provided by Christ is not a long way off from man; in natural temporal terms, it is *"...near...".*

> "The righteousness of faith speaks in this way, 'Do not say in your heart, 'Who will ascend into heaven?' (that is, to bring Christ down from above) or, 'Who will descend into the abyss?' (that is, to bring Christ up from

Birthed into the Supernatural

> *the dead". But what does it say? The word is near you, in your mouth and in your heart (that is, the word of faith which we preach): that if you confess with your mouth the Lord Jesus and believe in your heart that God has raised Him from the dead, you will be saved. For with the heart one believes unto righteousness, and with the mouth confession is made unto salvation."*
> **Romans 10:6-10**

When Christ is preached to the unsaved living in the natural world, whoever is preaching is actually introducing them to the Lord who is living in the spiritual world, in affect restoring the supernatural bridge which existed for Adam between the natural world and the spiritual world. If the lost will receive Jesus as the means to be saved, then God grants them right of access to the *"...eternal redemption..."!* By being born again man is *"...birthed...."* into the spiritual world.

> *"...As many as received Him, to them He gave the right to become children of God, to those who believe in His name: who were born, not of blood, nor of the will of the flesh, nor of the will of man, but of God..."* **John 1:12,13**

Man is not only born again. Paul told the church at Colosse...

> *"...He (the Father) has delivered us from the power of darkness and conveyed us into the kingdom of the Son of His love..."* **Colossians 1:13**

This *"...conveyance..."* is not primarily a geographic move but, rather, a restoration of the link with the spiritual world Adam lost. The Father *"...conveys..."* us into the invisible Kingdom of Christ and links us with the Lord by baptizing us into Him *(Romans 6:1-6; Galatians 3:26-29; I Corinthians 12:12,13)* making us *"...members of His body, of His flesh and of His bones..." (Ephesians 5:30)* as our abode *(John 15:1-8)*!

Eternal Fundamentals

Understanding these things is extremely important for at least two reasons: Firstly, because our God loves us and desires for us to know He and His provisions are not a long way off; they are near. Secondly, because He desires for us to understand the way of His kingdom!

We have already gained two profoundly significant understandings *(Chapter Four)*:

1. What Adam lost was not primarily dominion and possessions; *it was intimate relationship with God!* It was out of intimacy with God the first Adam had been designed to have dominion and possessions.

2. Jesus lived the life He lived and did the works He did by living in the Father and the Father living in Him. We will live like Jesus lived and do the works Jesus did by living in Christ and having the Christ live in us. Intimate relationship with the Christ is the priority of our faith, *"...not doing supernaturally mighty works..."!* Supernaturally mighty works will be *"...by-products..."* of our relationship with Christ Jesus!

Adam knew no separation between the natural and the spiritual: *He could see, hear, understand, and have intimate relationship with God!* After Adam's disobedience and subsequent expulsion from the Garden of Eden, a separation occurred. God was still close to Adam, only separated. God is near to everyone and everything all the time as a result of His divine *"...omnipresence..."*. David wrote...

> *"Where can I go from Your Spirit? Or where can I flee from Your presence? If I ascend into heaven, You are there; if I make my bed in hell, behold, You are there."*
> ***Psalms 139:7,8***

Birthed into the Supernatural

We have already seen how a revelation of God can be near to people but separated from their sight by only a *"...veil..." (Chapter Five)*. We saw this when Paul wrote about the concept of *"...veils..."* in comparing old covenant ministry with new covenant ministry. In this comparison he wrote, Moses *"...put a veil over his face so that the children of Israel could not look steadily at the end of what was passing away..." (II Corinthians 3:13)*. However, even though Moses is now dead, the veil is no longer on the *"...face..."* of the one who reads Moses today.

Paul wrote *"...even to this day, when Moses **is read, a veil lies on their heart**. Nevertheless when one turns to the Lord, the veil is taken away..." (II Corinthians 3:15-16)*. In this illustration it is easy to see the *"...veil..."* is what keeps people from seeing some particular revelation of God. Whether the veil is on the face of the one who reads Moses or the hearer's heart, it is still only a *"...veil..."* which keeps the revelation from being seen even though it is near.

The two completely separate environments of the earth and the sea have different rules governing life in each. Fish cannot live on land as do deer, and deer cannot live in the sea as do fish. In a parallel manner the two completely separate environments of the natural world and the spiritual world have different rules governing life in each.

Although we continue to use Nicodemus to illustrate man's inability to understand the things of the *"...spiritual world...",* we need to use him as illustration once again. Nicodemus, *"...a ruler of the Jews..." (John 3:1)*, a man of stature

Eternal Fundamentals

in the natural world, desired to understand the things Jesus was teaching but could not. Jesus told Nicodemus *"...unless one is born again, he cannot see the kingdom of God..." (John 3:3)*. Nicodemus began to apply the rules of the natural world in an effort to understand what Jesus just told him which was only able to be seen as a result of being born again. **Nicodemus was limited to the rules of the natural world, but why?**

> *"Nicodemus said to Him, 'How can a man be born when he is old? Can he enter a second time into his mother's womb and be born?" John 3:4*

Jesus' response demonstrated wonderful *"...stewardship..."*, endeavoring to *"...help..."* Nicodemus understand there are two completely separate environments in which birth can occur.

> *"Jesus answered, 'Most assuredly, I say to you, unless one is born of water and the Spirit, he cannot enter the kingdom of God. That which is born of the flesh is flesh, and that which is born of the Spirit is spirit. Do not marvel that I said to you, 'You must be born again.' The wind blows where it wishes, and you hear the sound of it, but cannot tell where it comes from and where it goes. So is everyone who is born of the Spirit." John 3:5-8*

Nicodemus' *"...unbelief..."* limited his sight to the rules of the natural world causing Jesus to give us a glimpse into His heart regarding fundamentals of relationship with God we desperately need today.

> *"Nicodemus answered and said to Him, 'How can these things be?' Jesus answered and said to him, 'Are you the teacher of Israel, and do not know these things? Most*

Birthed into the Supernatural

assuredly, I say to you, We speak what We know and testify what We have seen, and you do not receive Our witness. If I have told you earthly things and you do not believe, how will you believe if I tell you heavenly things?

John 3:9-12

These fundamentals can more easily be seen in Mary's encounter with the angel Gabriel. We can then compare her response with Nicodemus' response. Luke introduced Mary's experience in two verses *(Luke 1:26,27)* and recorded the entire encounter in the following ten verses of Scripture *(Luke 1:28-38)*. Within this brief moment in time, the angel Gabriel greeted Mary, made a few verbal exchanges including some questions and answers, Mary responded to the word Gabriel brought her from God, and it was over.

> *"Rejoice, highly favored one, the Lord is with you; blessed are you among women?' But when she saw him, she was troubled at his saying, and considered what manner of greeting this was. Then the angel said to her, 'Do not be afraid, Mary, for you have found favor with God, and behold, you will conceive in your womb and bring forth a Son, and shall call His name Jesus. He will be great, and will be called the Son of the Highest; and the Lord God will give Him the throne of His father David. And He will reign over the house of Jacob forever, and of His kingdom there will be no end. Then Mary said to the angel, 'How can this be, since I do not know a man?' And the angel answered and said to her, 'The Holy Spirit will come upon you, and the power of the Highest will overshadow you; therefore, also, that Holy One who is to be born will be called the Son of God. Now indeed, Elizabeth your relative has also conceived a son in her old age; and this is now the sixth month for her who was called barren. For with God nothing will be impossible. Then Mary said, 'Behold the maidservant of the Lord!*

Eternal Fundamentals

Let it be to me according to your word.' And the angel departed from her." **Luke 1:28-38**

How did Mary make such a life changing decision within the short space of time of this brief encounter? Was she just a foolish young woman without much world experience who did not know any better? Did God cause her to respond as she did by supernatural means? Shouldn't she have at least gone home to think or pray about it? Maybe her situation is completely different from Nicodemus' or ours? Maybe the *"...virgin birth..."* was just so important God took control? The answer to any and all of these questions leaves us lacking. There is something about Mary's encounter with the angel Gabriel that provides us with fundamental understanding regarding successful relationship development with God in the new covenant. **What is it?**

We find our first clue in **Luke 1:28,29**. Mary both *"...saw..."* the angel Gabriel and *"...heard..."* his voice. There are other Scriptures written about similar spiritual manifestations made available to natural man from the spiritual world. One such Scripture in which John recorded Jesus speaking about His impending death, God *"...spoke..."* from heaven. Nevertheless, those who heard the voice of God thought it thundered.

> *"Now My soul is troubled, and what shall I say? 'Father, save Me from this hour'? But for this purpose I came to this hour. Father, glorify Your name." Then a voice came from heaven, saying, 'I have both glorified it and will glorify it again. Therefore the people who stood by and heard it said that it had thundered."*
> ***John 12:27-29***

Birthed into the Supernatural

Because of the first Adam's disobedience, separation occurred between the natural and the spiritual for all man-kind. Even though the proximity of the temporal and the eternal is really close, there is a *"...veil..."* on the heart of natural man keeping him from participating in the provisions of God from the invisible world. Jesus as the last Adam came to restore what the first Adam lost *(Romans 5:12-21 & I Corinthians 15:35-49)*. Because of the last Adam's obedience a supernatural bridge is made available to whomsoever wills restoring the link between man and God and giving man opportunity to participate in provisions from the spiritual world.

We have already seen earlier in this chapter *"The two completely separate environments of the earth and the sea have different rules governing life in each. Fish cannot live on land as do deer, and deer cannot live in the sea as do fish. In a parallel manner the two completely separate environments of the natural world and the spiritual world have different rules governing life in each."*. Natural man experiences the natural world with five senses of sight, smell, taste, touch, and hearing. These five senses have rules governing them. *Webster's New Universal Unabridged Dictionary* defines *"...rules.."* as *"...established guides or regulations for action, conduct, method, arrangement, etc..."*.

For example, natural sight restricted to the natural world is available to man through the human eye. Man has learned certain rules governing how the eye works. If a malady or accident damages or destroys the eye, man's sight will be limited or removed altogether. Understanding the rules govern-

Eternal Fundamentals

ing natural *"...sight..."* has allowed man to discover ways to enhance this sense if it is diminished for some reason *(...age, malady, or injury...).* Understanding the rules governing all the natural senses has helped man more successfully access and experience the natural world.

Natural abilities are exclusive to the natural world. Only spiritual abilities can access the spiritual world. We need to understand what spiritual senses we have and the rules that govern them in order to experience the spiritual world successfully.

At the conclusion of certain times of ministry Jesus said, *"He who has ears to hear, let him hear!" (Matthew 11:15; Mark 4:9,23; Mark 7:16; Luke 8:8; Luke 14:35)* . Although Jesus was speaking to everyone in the crowd, He must not have believed everyone *"...(had) ears to hear..."*. According to Jesus' saying, *"He who has ears to hear, let him hear!"*, we begin to understand the ability to hear spiritual things must require more than just natural ears. Jesus is leading us to understand it takes more than natural senses to partake of things from the spiritual world.

Paul was inspired to consider how man experiences provisions from the spiritual world in his letter to the church at Corinth.

> *"Eye has not seen, nor ear heard, nor have entered into the heart of man the things which God has prepared for those who love Him. But God has revealed them to us through His Spirit. For the Spirit searches all things, yes, the deep things of God. For what man knows the things of a man except the spirit of the man which is in him? Even so no one knows the things of God except*

the Spirit of God. Now we have received, not the spirit of the world, but the Spirit who is from God, that we might know the things that have been freely given to us by God. These things we also speak, not in words which man's wisdom teaches but which the Holy Spirit teaches, comparing spiritual things with spiritual. But the natural man does not receive the things of the Spirit of God, for they are foolishness to him; nor can he know them, because they are spiritually discerned."

I Corinthians 2:9-14

In the context immediately before and after this portion of Scripture Paul contrasted natural with spiritual as applied to a person who is born again. In *I Corinthians 2:14* the Holy Spirit is teaching us *"...the natural man does not receive the things of the Spirit of God, for they are foolishness to him; nor can he know them, because they are spiritually discerned..."*. That is, man cannot know the things of the Spirit of God with his natural senses.

We have already considered the account of Paul in Rome under house arrest ministering to Jewish leaders *(Chapter One)*. However, it is valuable to reconsider the account here from another perspective. When Paul saw them disagreeing among themselves and some disbelieving, he applied a word to them which had been prophesied in a historical context by the prophet Isaiah :

"Go to this people and say: 'Hearing you will hear, and shall not understand; and seeing you will see, and not perceive; for the hearts of this people have grown dull. Their ears are hard of hearing, and their eyes they have closed, lest they should see with their eyes and hear with their ears, lest they should understand with their hearts and turn, so that I should heal them.'..."

Romans 28:26,27

Eternal Fundamentals

Isaiah's original prophesy and Paul's current application of it to these Jewish leaders is very similar to Jesus' saying, *"He who has ears, let him hear!"*. Jesus' words helped us begin to understand He was not referring to natural ears and natural hearing. When Isaiah prophesied saying the people were unable to *"...see..."*, *"...hear..."*, or *"...understand..."* he, too, was not referring to their natural abilities. Neither was Paul when he quoted Isaiah's prophesy applying it to the Jewish leaders to whom he was ministering. Jesus, Isaiah, and Paul knew the people had functional natural eyes and ears, yet these ministers of God used the terms *"...see..."* and *"...hear..."* in relation to people gaining spiritual understanding.

Sight and hearing are not only natural senses, they are also spiritual senses. Natural sight and hearing are unique to natural man so he may be able to see and hear in the natural world. Spiritual sight and hearing are unique to spiritual man so he may be able to see and hear in the spiritual world. Sight and hearing are not two senses interchangeable between the natural world and the spiritual world. Natural sight and natural hearing cannot be used to see and hear in the spiritual world. Spiritual sight and spiritual hearing always present in man were restricted by Adam's disobedience. At the time of new birth the restriction is removed giving man opportunity to see and hear God's provisions from the spiritual world, however, man can cause a *"...veil..."* to be on his heart so he cannot see or hear.

We have already seen *(Chapter Five)* in Paul's second letter to the church at Corinth his consideration of *"...veils..."*. This illustration provides us with three important understandings:

Birthed into the Supernatural

1. **The first:** Moses introduced the veil by placing it over his own face to keep the people from seeing revelation he had received while in the presence of God *(Exodus 34:29-35 & II Corinthians 3:13)*. Something small enough to be called a *"...veil..."* only covering Moses' face stopped the people from beholding revelation from God.

2. **The second:** Moses determined the veil would be placed over his own face to keep the people from seeing revelation from God but, afterward, the condition of the peoples' heart controlled the placement of the veil to be over their own heart *(II Corinthians 3: 15)*.

3. **The third:** If a person will *"...turn to the Lord, the veil is taken away..." (II Corinthians 3:16)* so they can see God's provisions in the spiritual world.

Two of these understandings help us see a rule governing our spiritual senses: *Our heart regulates our spiritual sight and hearing.* If our heart is not turned toward the Lord, the restriction established by Adam's disobedience together with our own unwillingness to do the will of God remains in place. This causes a veil to be on our own heart keeping us from seeing and hearing God's provisions in the spiritual world. If our heart will turn toward the Lord, the restriction will be removed, and we will be able to see and hear God's provisions.

The exquisitely simple difference between Mary and Nicodemus was the condition of the heart of each. Mary's heart was turned toward the Lord, believing in God. Any veil which may have restricted her was removed. Nicodemus was limited to understanding based on the rules governing the natural world because of the unbelief in his heart. This veil kept him from *"...seeing..."* the glorious provision of God in the invisible world, even though it was Jesus Himself endeavoring to show it to him. The only prerequisite necessary for a person to enter into and develop relationship with God and to have the link to God's provisions in the spiritual world restored is for the person to turn his heart toward God. According to Scripture when a person turns his heart toward the Lord, *"...veils..."* will be removed and the person will behold the provision of God *(II Corinthians 3:16-18)*.

Gabriel greeted Mary with... *"...highly favored one, the Lord is with you..." (Luke 1:28)*. Mary's heart was turned toward her God allowing the link to the spiritual world to be restored for her so she could see and hear God's provision for her. When the angel Gabriel appeared and spoke to her, she both *"...saw..."* and *"...heard..."* him because of the condition of her heart. From the very beginning of the encounter Mary understood this was provision from her God.

How does a person allow the spiritual eternal to take precedence over his natural temporal life? **Keep your heart turned toward the Lord!** Scripture teaches...

> *"...For those who live according to the flesh set their minds on the things of the flesh, but those who live according to the Spirit, the things of the Spirit. For to be carnally minded is death, but to be spiritually minded is life and peace. Because the carnal mind is enmity against God; for it is not subject to the law of God, nor indeed can be..."* **Romans 8:5-7**

Birthed into the Supernatural

Eternal is greater than and has precedence over the temporal. Our natural lives are temporal; our spiritual lives are eternal. Jesus said, *"...seek first the kingdom of God and His righteousness..." (Matthew 6:33)*, establishing the priority of our lives: Eternal first! We can, and must, apply this understanding to our senses.

Our natural senses are temporal; our spiritual senses are eternal. One of the devices of the enemy is to attempt to deceive us into believing our natural senses are greater than our eternal senses. However, God predicated our salvation on *"...faith..." (Ephesians 2:8,9)*. Paul wrote in his second letter to the church at Corinth, *"...we walk by faith, not by sight..." (II Corinthians 5:7)*. The old covenant did not produce the results God desired because it was based on man's ability to do the will of God *(Romans 8:1-4; Hebrews 8:7,13)*. The new covenant is based on man doing the will of God in *"...faith..." (...the ability God provides...)!* God's way is better than man's way!

No matter how well a person may be able to see and hear with his natural sight and hearing, neither sense can compare to man's spiritual sight and hearing. Man does not *"...see..."* God's provisions with his natural eye, nor does he *"...hear..."* God's provisions with his natural ear. It should be noted that God can sovereignly cause man to both see and hear His provisions with his natural eye and ear. However, such a choice is an exception to the *"...rules..."* governing spiritual sight and spiritual hearing, done only at the discretion of God and His sovereign will. Otherwise, we are to use our spiritual sight to see and our spiritual hearing to hear God's provisions from the spiritual eternal world.

Conclusion

Have you ever planned an event only to find at the time of the actual event you forgot a necessary ingredient? Maybe you planned a back yard cook out inviting family and friends, but when they arrived, you discovered you forgot to replenish the charcoal. Maybe you planned a fishing trip, arrived at the stream you planned on fishing, only to discover you forgot your waders. Maybe you planned to cut the grass on a particular day, but when the day came, you discovered you were out of gas. All of us have fallen victim to such things.

However, when our God planned to redeem us, He did not forget a single thing. His plans were perfect! There were no *"...oops..."* in God's plans! His provisions and timing were impeccable! Jesus' crucifixion and death, while grotesque to our natural senses, were carefully planned in the power of divine attributes as the only means to redeem us.

Consider all of the intricacies involved leading up to the cross: finding a virgin who had favor with God willing to participate in the plan of God, finding a man who would yield to God when his betrothed told him she was pregnant as a virgin, the baby Jesus escaping Herod's evil decree to *"...put to death all the male children who were in Bethlehem and in all its districts, from two years old and under..." (**Matthew 2:16**)*, Jesus divesting Himself of His divine attributes living on earth as a man free of sin, Jesus' willingness to actually partake of the sufferings and death of the cross. There are just too many things to know or consider that were part of God's plan to redeem us.

Birthed into the Supernatural

It is true all things involved in the plan to redeem us required the power of God to bring them to pass. However, God's power did not force Mary to conceive; she had to be willing to yield to God and His plan for her. God did not force Joseph to take Mary to be his wife; he had to yield to the knowledge God gave him about Mary's immaculate conception. God did not force Jesus to suffer and die for us; Jesus had to yield to the plan of God as an act of His own free will.

Contrary to the device with which the enemy is constantly trying to deceive us, God is not in control of our choices! If God were in control, then every time we fall short, He chose for us to fall short. We are not Pinocchio, and God is not Geppetto! God is not pulling strings on us as if we were His puppets. We have a will, and we make the choices by which we live. Mary, Joseph, and Jesus all three had wills with which they chose. God did not sovereignly override their wills to bring to pass the events of their lives

Considering all these things from the perspective they have been presented, is there any way you can imagine God conceiving and executing His plan to redeem us but forgetting to make a way for us to *"...live..."* redeemed? As extraordinary, even unbelievable as it is, God wills for us to live like Jesus and to do the works Jesus did! We will do these things in exactly the same principle manner as Mary, Joseph, or Jesus. He will make His will known to us giving us opportunity to yield to it, but we must choose to yield or not.

Living like Jesus lived and doing the works Jesus did are both expectations of God which must be developed. A natural father does not hand his car keys to his newborn son

Conclusion

expecting him to drive to the corner market to pick up bread and milk. Neither does Abba expect us as newborn babes in Christ to immediately walk as mature sons of God! It seems so foolish to ask, but do you think God does not understand the maturation process required for an *"...infant..."* to grow up *"...to a perfect man, to the measure of the stature of the fullness of Christ..." (Ephesians 4:13)?*

The process from new birth to maturity in Christ has become so obscure, it is as if it no longer exists. In the natural world we have so many tools to help us monitor a child's development, involving both rewards and consequences. In the spiritual world it is as if monitoring a person who has been born again has been rejected altogether. The general consensus seems to be our lives and the choices of our lives are between just us and God.

I remember living with my wife and two small children in a grass house in a mangrove swamp in a remote village of Papua New Guinea. It was time to teach one of our children to pray. We asked our daughter to pray over a meal. She prayed, *"Thank you Father for me and Jesus, for me and mommy, for me and daddy, for me and the food."* Immediately, the Holy Spirit asked me if I believed our child was praying in a selfish manner. I did not believe she was praying in a selfish manner, but I also believed the Holy Spirit desired to teach me something using her prayer, so I just answered, *"No"*. The Holy Spirit said, *"Your child is not being selfish. She is merely learning to establish her identity in relation to others in her life and to become secure in who she is. If she does not learn her true identity and become secure in it, she will not be able to take her rightful place in life."*

Birthed into the Supernatural

In exactly the same way, every newborn in Christ must learn who he is in Christ and who Christ is in Him! He must learn the way of the kingdom into which he has been birthed. The child does not do that by himself. He must be overseen just as a natural child requires oversight. The church on the earth is living today in what has been the way of the church for generations. We must not be afraid to examine that way in order to determine if it is truly the way of the Lord! Questions we must ask and answer are simple: Are we living like Jesus lived, and are we doing the works He did? If the answers to these questions are negative, then we must begin to ask, seek, and knock to find God's solutions.

> *"For I say, through the grace given to me, to everyone who is among you, not to think of himself more highly than he ought to think, but to think soberly, as God has dealt to each one a measure of faith."* **Romans 12:3**

www.ingramcontent.com/pod-product-compliance
Lightning Source LLC
Chambersburg PA
CBHW071310040426
42444CB00009B/1966